UNTYING THE KNOT

UNTYING THE KNOT
Working with
Children and Parents

A. H. Brafman

For Roger Willoughby
with Thanks for your
interest + support.

[signature]

6.7.01

London & New York
KARNAC BOOKS

First published in 2001 by
H. Karnac (Books) Ltd.
6 Pembroke Buildings, London NW10 6RE

A subsidiary of Other Press LLC, New York

British Library Cataloguing in Publication Data

A C.I.P. for this book is available from the British Library

ISBN 1 85575 255 7

10 9 8 7 6 5 4 3 2 1

Edited, designed, and produced by Communication Crafts

www.karnacbooks.com

Printed in Great Britain by Biddles Short Run Books, King's Lynn

I would like to express my gratitude to the children and parents who made this book possible: I learnt a great deal from them, and I hope they found some help in our joint venture.

I am also grateful to Cesare Sacerdoti for his valuable encouragement to produce this book and to Marcus Johns who made it possible for this work to first come into print. To Rosine J. Perelberg, a sincere "obrigado" for her faithful support.

Above all, my thanks to Lilian and our growing family, without whose love and inspiration this book would not have come into being.

CONTENTS

CHAPTER ONE
Introduction   1

CHAPTER TWO
The clinical encounter   11

CHAPTER THREE
Child and parent interacting   47

CHAPTER FOUR
Mainly the child   95

CHAPTER FIVE
Virtually only the child   123

CHAPTER SIX
Summing up   155

REFERENCES   161

INDEX   162

UNTYING THE KNOT

Introduction

Psychoanalytic theory and practice focus exclusively on the psyche of the individual. In the course of the decades since Freud's fundamental discoveries, there has been a proliferation of theories and techniques and a multiplication of names to describe them. At the start of the new millennium, psychoanalysis *sensu strictu* has become a respected body of theories, but its clinical application appears to be restricted to training purposes and the treatment of an ever-decreasing number of patients. "Psychoanalytic psychotherapy" is now more prevalent, and this seems to encompass a large number of treatment modalities whose common elements can, at times, be difficult to distinguish.

Two of the main therapeutic offshoots of psychoanalytic theories have been the application of its principles to the treatment of children and of groups. Each has yielded a rich field of new concepts and techniques, but, in broad terms, child psychotherapy still focuses on the psyche of the individual child, whereas group approaches unravel the dynamics of individuals having to associate with others. Not surprisingly, the family also came to be put under the analytic microscope, and, since the 1940s, family therapy has carved out its own territory. Initially, it was the families of schizophrenics who were studied, and soon enough parents who were supposedly "normal" came to be described as having a powerful influence on the development of the psychotic picture of the pre-senting patient. At about the same time, child psychiatrists also brought the children's parents under clinical scrutiny, but some-how it came to be very rare that these approaches paid sufficient attention to the child's experience of the family life. This may well have been due to the fact that most therapists were used to work-ing with adults, and, depending on the child's age and capacity to articulate his thoughts,* it was simply easier to concentrate on the adults.

This book sets out to present a clinical approach to cases where the referred patient is a child or adolescent, but the parents are intimately involved in the therapeutic intervention. Three funda-mental principles guide the work: (1) our present life is influenced by earlier experiences; (2) our behaviour and conscious life is influ-enced by our unconscious feelings and fantasies; and (3) child and parents influence each other in such a way that it may be impossi-ble to establish what is cause and what is effect in their interactions.

I have often used Winnicott's term "therapeutic consultation" to describe the case studies presented in this book. This is not just because most of the children were seen only once or twice, but also because I was following his approach and many of his concepts, which I find very convincing. As will be seen, I have developed my own way of dealing with children and their parents in this work, but my debt to Winnicott cannot be emphasized enough. It is his respect for the child as an individual that singles him out from many other professionals. His wish to help the child had nothing to do with the doctor's sense of pride in defeating illness or the scien-tist's triumph in finding confirmation for his or her theories, but, instead, it seemed to flow from his desire to bring relief to the child and make it again happy, well functioning, and moving towards independence and self-sufficiency. In other words, his commit-ment was to the child and not to his theoretical convictions. It is a model worth adopting.

---

*For the sake of simplicity, in general discussions masculine pronouns are used for patients and for analysts.

Winnicott made valuable contributions to several clinical areas. Besides seeing "ordinary" neurotic patients, his work with psychotic and borderline patients set standards that are respected and followed; in addition, his experience in paediatrics, child psychiatry, and child analysis meant that he had contact with thousands of infants, children, and adolescents, whom he followed very closely for extended periods in different clinical and social settings. These parallel fields of work meant that, while other analysts conceptualized human emotional development on the basis of inferences from their work with adults, Winnicott could draw on his extensive experience with babies and young children to put forward an object-relations developmental theory that is particularly persuasive. Some of the concepts arising from the body of his theoretical framework have become part of the everyday vocabulary of most practitioners in the caring professions—for example, the "good-enough mother", the "average expectable environment", "transitional objects", the "holding environment", and the "antisocial tendency". Considering how his theoretical concepts are so widely accepted, it is puzzling to find that Winnicott's accounts of his actual, clinical work with very regressed patients and with children in his hospital clinics tend to be seen as reflections of his personal attributes—that is, not so easy to be put into practice by other professionals.

Discussing the diagnostic consultations with children that had produced therapeutic results, Winnicott defined their motto (his word) as "How little need be done (to help the child)?", whilst in psychoanalysis, he wrote, the motto was "How much may the analyst be allowed to do?"* I believe he was referring to the ever-increasing length of psychoanalytic therapies and the rationale for this approach. Since Freud's warning (1910) against the misleading results of brief therapeutic interventions based on false or premature interpretations of psychoanalytic concepts, psychoanalysts had taken the length of treatment and the frequency of interviews as yardsticks of the validity and effectiveness of the therapy. Winnicott himself had had lengthy analyses, and this might have influenced his formulation. It is also possible that he might be

---

*From a summary sheet distributed at a presentation given by Winnicott to the British Psycho-Analytical Society on 7 July 1965.

referring to the concept of psychoanalysis as an instrument of research into the workings of the human mind; as such, however long the therapy, there would always be something further to put under scrutiny. From all these points of view, Winnicott's formulation rightly emphasized the importance of the consultant being able to balance out patients' needs and wishes against his own view of what treatment he might want to recommend. Winnicott's contrast of the two clinical options is a succinct summary of the complex range of factors that influence the consultant's eventual advice to the patient regarding the decision they must, together, make on how to proceed.

Because of his medical training, Winnicott would be intensely aware of the steps followed by every doctor when seeing a new patient: clinical examination, differential diagnosis, consideration of different therapeutic interventions, and prognostic evaluation of each of these—and only then the decision as to which therapy to prescribe. The complexity of the problem of finding the best compromise between the doctor's view of the *ideal* treatment and the patient's wish for immediate cure is part of every doctor's daily life. The decision to recommend long-term psychoanalysis or psychotherapy may derive from recognizing that this is the treatment modality most beneficial to the patient, or, occasionally, consultant and patient will agree to study in detail the psychopathology underlying the patient's problems; however, at times this decision may result from the consultant's *a priori* belief that only a prolonged, intensive therapy may be able to bring to that patient the relief he seeks. This latter viewpoint would move from discernment and judgement towards the biased statement of faith. I suspect that it is this approach to the issue of "helping" and "healing" that Winnicott had in mind when he formulated his two mottoes. I believe he was trying to call his colleagues' attention to the existence of therapeutic options and, hopefully, get them to accept the fact that many children can benefit from brief psychotherapeutic interventions.

Implied in Winnicott's phrase is the reminder that, first and foremost, children come to us hoping to find relief, to find help with their problems. Meeting a new child patient, Winnicott's first concern was to make a diagnostic evaluation of the child's physical and emotional development. Before deciding on the actual therapeutic intervention, Winnicott assessed the parents' capacity to offer the child the environmental provisions that he considered necessary—and only then did he decide whether the child could benefit from a brief intervention or whether, instead, the child required a more long-term therapeutic input. In practice, these stages tend to blend into each other, and perhaps they are not so easily identifiable as I have defined them; however, this sequence constitutes a valid philosophy of work, and it has served as my model, as will be seen.

History: Winnicott

Winnicott's book *Therapeutic Consultations in Child Psychiatry* was published in 1971. In the Introduction to the book he emphasized that his aim was not to present cases illustrating symptomatic cure, but, rather, to report "examples of *communication with children*" (emphasis in original). This formulation probably followed from Winnicott's awareness that his psychoanalytic colleagues viewed with suspicion, if not open disapproval, his claims of therapeutic results in the course of brief clinical interviews. Psychoanalysts were moving towards ever more prolonged analyses, and any attempts to shorten the treatment of people with emotional problems were viewed with mistrust. This is particularly surprising when no reader of that book can fail to marvel at the beneficial results following from Winnicott understanding the child's "communication" and putting this into words for the child.

Winnicott never conducted his therapeutic consultations with the aim of demonstrating his virtuosity or to obtain quick results in his work with children. He was a clinician of exceptional sensitivity, and he had the capacity to recognize new findings and proceed to explore them rather than to explain them away by turning to some accepted dogma. Having found that a diagnostic interview could produce clear, dramatic improvement, he must have decided to investigate further whether this was an isolated, fortuitous good result or whether this could be duplicated with other children. As it turned out, he went on to find a large number of similar successful consultations, some of which are reported in that book.

Therapeutic Consultations (1971b) can be read in many different ways. The clinical cases are vividly described, and they represent fascinating reading, even if read as no more than interesting stories. The "Squiggle Game" that Winnicott employed in the cases described is a most effective way of bringing to light the child's unconscious conflicts, and Winnicott cannot be contradicted in his claim that the game is a valuable way of "communicating with children". The finding of significant improvement in the child after one or a few interviews poses a challenge to the clinician, but even more so to the theoretician who might want to discover the rationale for the changes experienced and presented by the child. Critically minded therapists have plenty of clinical material that they can use in order to argue how they would have preferred to deal with a particular child. Professionals who work with children have much to learn from Winnicott's account of how he approached and engaged the child. Considering the many different ways of learning from this book, it must be surprising to find that there have been recurring criticisms of Winnicott's therapeutic consultations. These were aptly summarized by Phillips (1988): "there was something 'magical', his critics thought, in the fluency of his contact with the children he saw, as though all one could learn from his clinical accounts was that one was unable to be Winnicott" (p. 16).

Winnicott certainly had a unique capacity to tune in to his patients' wavelength, and this comes across in all his clinical accounts, both when working with children and with adults. But I tend to think that the "magic" that many critics picked on is probably linked to the objective pursued when meeting the child. Most practitioners will approach the child with the goal of identifying the child's suitability for a particular treatment; many will attempt a diagnostic evaluation, where data are gathered to match different categories—but as I understand him, Winnicott set out to find the *nature of the child's experience* of his problem, which is a goal that has many important implications. Much as in any similar situation, the answer one finds is influenced by the question or task one sets out to resolve, and, even more important, the consultant's utterances and emotional posture are profoundly influenced by his aim in addressing the patient. Gathering data does not require any emotional involvement, since "a sympathetic attitude" of professionalism is considered sufficient to gain the confidence of most patients, whatever their age. When the consultant wants to learn the nature of the problems experienced by the patient—that is, not just "the facts", but what the patient believes afflicts him—this is interpreted by the patient as a warm, humane personal interest in how he feels. Winnicott knew how to convey to the child his readiness and desire to make deep emotional contact, and it is this mutual coming together that probably gave readers and outsiders (Winnicott usually had visitors attending his consultations) the impression of something magical.

The cases described in Winnicott's book (1971b) show that identifying the specific unconscious fantasy underlying the child's symptoms brought about a resolution of these conflicts—and, at this point, an altogether different question comes to the fore: is this relief enough? Or does the child need more help/treatment? Those who believe that only treatment that is prolonged and "deep" can claim true psychotherapeutic value dismissed Winnicott's interventions as superficial and not truly effective. Analysts and therapists who worked in National Health Service clinics, and who had learnt to adapt their psychoanalytic knowledge to the constraints of the facilities available, could recognize the advantages of Winnicott's approach, but, on the whole, whether they applied the squiggle game or not, most of these therapists considered their consultations exclusively a diagnostic tool: preference was still given to the prescription of long-term, individual or family therapy.

The present book presents a number of cases where children were seen along similar principles to those described by Winnicott: they were children referred for a diagnostic assessment, which eventually turned out to be a therapeutically effective intervention. But I hope to show the advantage of including the child's parents in these meetings. This departs from Winnicott's definition of the parents' role in the child's treatment, and I discuss the clinical and theoretical implications of this closer scrutiny of the parents' relationship to the child.

The squiggle game played a central role in Winnicott's cases. After an apparently brief introduction during which he made the child feel at ease and settled into a comfortable position, sitting near him around a table where paper and pencils were available, he proposed to the child that they should play a game. This entailed a sequence of drawings in which Winnicott made an impromptu, meaningless doodle and asked the child to transform it into anything at all; most, if not all, children responded to this without difficulty. Winnicott went on talking to the child, continuing their previous conversation, but he now asked the child to make a squiggle, which he, Winnicott, proceeded to transform into whatever it was that he "saw" in the child's squiggle. As they continued the drawings, it could be seen that the child and Winnicott had isolated themselves from people and things around them and were now engaged in a close, intimate relationship where words and drawings complemented each other. At some point of the sequence the child would notice that a picture he had drawn represented or reminded him of a dream, and Winnicott discovered that this dream presented the necessary clues to recognize the unconscious fantasy that underlay the child's presenting problems. I imagine Winnicott was surprised when he first discovered that the articulation of this unconscious fantasy brought about such a dramatic improvement in the child, but it seems that he came to expect similar results with later cases.

The parents did not take part in the interviews. Winnicott's accounts convey vividly the child's growing trust and closeness, gradually becoming immersed in the game, as if entering into a special kind of contact with Winnicott, where the child's conscious vigilance appeared to be suspended and his unconscious seemed to come to the fore. Winnicott postulated that when this closeness occurred, the child was not relating to him, the doctor sitting down next to the child, but to some figure that seemed to be part of the child's internal unconscious world: "here I was, as I discovered to my amusement, *fitting in with a preconceived notion*. The children who had dreamed in this way were able to tell me that it was of me that they had dreamed. In language which I use now, but which I had no equipment for using at that time, I found myself in the role of subjective object" (Winnicott, 1971b, p. 4; emphasis in original). In other words, the child was turning to Winnicott as the person (object) in the outside world who would embody the attributes of that ideal helper he had dreamt of and who would, therefore, be able to understand his problems and bring the relief he craved for.

Once the consultation was finished and Winnicott had discussed his interpretation with the child, he invited one or both parents to join them. It seems that early in his work he showed to the parents the drawings their child had made and shared with them what had transpired in the interview, but he must have found serious disappointments in this, since he writes of parents betraying his confidence ("Parents might perhaps abuse the confidence that the therapist has placed in them, and so undo the work that depends on a kind of intimacy between child and therapist": Winnicott, 1971b, p. 4). Beyond this particular aspect, he drew a distinction between parents who had the ability to support the child in building further on the initial improvement and other parents whose personality and/or social circumstances would not allow them to play this role. In the latter case, when parents were unable to give the child the protective care he needed, it was necessary to consider other therapeutic interventions:

> if the child goes away from the therapeutic consultation *and returns to an abnormal family or social situation* then there is no environmental provision of the kind that is needed and that I take for granted. I rely on an "average expectable environment" to meet and to make use of the changes that have taken place in the boy or girl in the interview, changes which indicate a loosening of the knot in the developmental process. ... Where there is a powerful continuing adverse external factor or an absence of consistent personal care, then one would avoid this kind of procedure and would feel inclined either to explore what could be done by "management" or else to institute a therapy which would give the child the opportunity for a personal relationship of the kind that is generally known as transference. [Winnicott, 1971b, pp. 5–6; emphasis in original]

In the work to be presented here, parents play a prominent role. Their active participation in the interviews allows us to have a first-hand view of how child and parents relate to each other, as well as giving us an opportunity to explore what the child's symptoms mean to each of them. The goal of identifying the child's unconscious fantasy underlying the symptom is still pursued, but an additional objective is the understanding of the factors operating in each parent which are related to the child's problems. In other words, these joint meetings give us an opportunity to understand each parent's role in the creation and/or persistence of the child's problems, as well as to gauge how much help each parent is, in fact, able to offer the child.

In chapter two, I discuss in more detail the various elements that have been mentioned in the overview in this chapter.

The clinical encounter

The child

We tend to assume that younger children are "brought" for help and older ones are "sent" by someone to see us, which might make for considerable uncertainty when we consider the issue of motivation for help and change. This question will seem quite different if we look at the "symptom" as a plea for help. Within the framework of individual psychopathology, the symptom constitutes a compromise between the unconscious impulse seeking gratification and the defensive forces that block this. If, instead, we look at the symptom as an indication that the child has been unable to solve some underlying internal conflict and is turning to his outside world seeking help, the symptom itself comes to represent a statement of motivation towards some less painful state of affairs. In this formulation, it is the parents whom the child first approaches, and, as we will see later on, their response will affect how the child progresses. When the child receives appropriate help from one or both parents, it is most unlikely that we will ever see him—a totally obvious statement that flows from the number of children who cope reasonably well with obstacles to their emotional development. When the parents cannot cope with the child's needs, there is a chance that in one of innumerable different ways, the child will come to the attention of someone outside the family circle. Winnicott discussed this issue at length in his work on the "antisocial tendency" (1956), in which he interprets antisocial behaviour as an attempt to reinstate or obtain again the care and love felt to have been lost at some point in the individual's development.

Sometimes, children are brought to see us because the parent is needing help for him/herself. What can make these cases extremely difficult to recognize is the fact that with some of these children "nothing can be found", while others do have "real problems". It is a good rule-of-thumb to assume that every child brought to us is living with a problem, and the challenge is to disentangle how much of this "problem" resides in the child and to what extent is this "problem" an indication that one or more people in the family are struggling with difficulties. The now well-known syndrome of Munchausen by proxy is only an extreme example of this dynamic configuration. Many children will develop symptoms as a response to the parent(s)' needs, and it is a common, but serious, mistake to focus only on the family or the relevant parent and ignore the child's own conflict. Even if we believe that the symptom is "caused" by the parent, the child will still have elaborated his perceptions of the parental conflict into his own unconscious fantasy, and the content of this fantasy needs to be elucidated for the child's benefit.

Winnicott's description of the children having seen him in their dreams (in spite of not having met him before), and the highly charged atmosphere of closeness that was created in the therapeutic consultations, both point to the child's belief that this was not just an ordinary stranger he was meeting, but a stranger who he hoped might bring him relief from his problems. This is one of the pieces of information that lead me to look at the child's symptom as being object-directed. On the other hand, we sometimes meet children of all ages who display intense anger and resentment at having to see us. On closer scrutiny, we can find that this protest is often directed at the parents, who, instead of proving the good parents who help the child themselves, decide to bring him to see the consultant. This is why it is rare to find a child who does not relent and adopt a more cooperative attitude towards the consultant. However much the child appears to oppose his parents' decision to consult a professional, the fact of their presence should justify an assumption that the child has an awareness that he and/or another member of the family needs help.

Most children who come to see a child psychiatrist, analyst, or therapist have no previous experience of that situation and they can only fall back on whatever earlier experience they manage to associate to that encounter. The child's expectations are intensely influenced by his parents' words, but the consultant cannot guess what explanation the child was given about coming to see him. What actually comes to happen depends on how the consultant conducts the meeting—for example, how child and parents are received and how they are offered seats in the consulting-room already contain many cues that the child has to interpret in order to understand what this new person—the consultant or therapist—expects from him. How the child makes his gradual progress throughout these apparently trivial details should give the consultant a rich view of the relationship between the child and his parents and also how the child is seeing the consultant.

Children (and all of us, I believe) can sense very quickly what a doctor is seeking to find in a meeting. It is part of the nature of a consultation that the consultant is seen as the "stage master", and patients will adapt to his directives with only occasional awareness of the implications and consequences created by that adaptation. The consultant will conduct his questions and comments in line with the objective he is pursuing—and the child will adapt to this, as will the parents as well. This is not a question of "which is the correct or the best approach", but, rather, an unavoidable sequence of events which demands that the consultant should be aware of the way in which he is influencing the responses of the patients. When I make a point of addressing the child first, as soon as the family have made themselves comfortable, I intend to convey the message that it is the child's experience of his problems that constitutes my main focus of attention. Parents are usually quite happy to sit back and follow the way in which the child deals with my questions. When one of them corrects or interrupts the child, I explain to them that it is not so important for me to learn "the correct facts", but to discover how the child interprets what goes on around him—and most parents will accept this as a cue to allow the child to proceed on his own.

How does one "engage" the child? I cannot recall being asked this question by students training in psychoanalysis or psychotherapy, but it comes up very frequently when I am seeing medical students. Strange as it may seem, I have also had parents asking me this question. Presumably, these are people who recognize a challenge that they do not know how to overcome. It took me some time to understand that trainees do not ask that question because they *believe* they know what to do. In fact, I discovered, they only knew what they *were supposed* to do. Analytic and therapy trainees have always had a first training, which might suggest that they are experienced in engaging their clients or, if this is the case, that they would know how to approach a child. But it became apparent that in their new role they believe they have to abandon their previous skills and, instead, adopt the posture of the "analyst". The trainees' usual view of this role is that of the "mirror analyst", the expert who interprets the unconscious meaning of what the patient does or fails to do, and, together with the rule of "free association" and a constant observation of "the transference", this is taken to mean that it is not for the trainee to put the patient at ease, to show an interest in the patient's comfort or to explain what exactly is expected of the patient.

With parents, this question becomes relevant when they say that the child "will never tell me anything!" Observing the interaction between these parents and their child, one can easily see that they are forever *telling* their children what they think; even when they ask a question, they will interrupt the child's answer and complete the child's sentence according to what they believe the child was going to say. With medical students, the topic comes up in a very similar manner: does the doctor ask a question and wait for a full answer, or does he promptly supply the answer he wants to hear? At stake is the issue of how interested is one party to discover what exactly the other party thinks or feels. It is not easy to explain this point without sounding critical or judgemental, so I often try another way of putting this point across. I ask the students or the parents to try to remember an occasion when they visited their GP's surgery and found that their own doctor was away, so that they were seen by another doctor, a situation that every single one of them has been through: "As you walk into the surgery, how long does it take you to decide whether this new doctor wants to discuss your situation with you or whether he just wants to give you a prescription?" They all laugh and try to quote some extremely brief interval of time. My argument is that this is what happens every time you meet a new patient, whatever his age, but much more dramatically so with children. Children very quickly sense what is being offered to them, and they will adapt to that particular perception they have of the person in front of them. Sadly, this same mechanism operates between children and their parents as well, and many children described as withdrawn or unreachable can be found to have an image of their parent(s) as people who are not interested in knowing what the child himself actually thinks or feels. One of the major advantages of seeing child and parents together is precisely the opportunity to verify whether this (conscious or unconscious) image of self-centred parents is a distortion created by the child's conflicts or, conversely, a correct perception of their attitudes towards the child.

I always begin by introducing myself. "Do you know who I am?" is a useful starting gambit. I proceed by taking the child's answer as a guide to his command of language and to what he wants to know and wants to tell me. After my name, I explain that, though I am a doctor, I will not be examining him physically, because my work is with children and/or adolescents who are unhappy or have some problem that bothers them. This is a good introduction to the question "Do you need someone like me?", which always makes the parents laugh and leads the child to relax and think what would be the best answer to give me. If the child just curls up, either embarrassed or afraid, I assume that the question was asked too prematurely, and I move on to subjects that are likely to arouse less anxiety.

School, family life, siblings, neighbours, friends, hobbies, and various interests are areas that children find very easy to discuss. After all these "neutral" subjects have been covered, the child will usually find it easier to tackle the question "Why are you here?" or "Why have your parents thought of bringing you to see me?" Their answers will help us gradually to develop an image of how they feel about themselves and what they make of the world in which they live. Throughout this dialogue, we can discern how the child relates to us, and this is a further datum in building that image of the child in his world. At one level, we are learning data, facts about the child's life, but on another level, we have to assess how the child has negotiated his developmental stages. His use of language, his general behaviour in the room and on the chair, his ability to differentiate between fantasy and reality, his capacity to recognize the boundary between self and other, as well as between different others, are some of the elements that will help us in our appraisal. The *content* of the child's answers will help us to understand his unconscious experience of all these events, people, relationships, and so forth, but we must remember that a diagnostic assessment must include a proper evaluation of the child's emotional, social, and cognitive development. (For example, I have seen patients with severe behaviour problems that I believed were the result of their adaptation to difficulties created by an undiagnosed learning difficulty.) The assessment of these features will rely mostly on the *formal* aspects of the child's speech and behaviour. Using different words, we have to understand *what* the child is saying, but we must also pay attention to *how* he says it.

Describing his therapeutic consultations, Winnicott wrote that they were

> special occasions that have a quality that has made me use the word sacred. Either this sacred moment is used or it is wasted. If it is wasted the child's belief in being understood is shattered. If on the other hand it is used, then the child's belief in being helped is strengthened. [1971b, pp. 4–5]

I remember being fascinated and full of admiration and envy when I first read these words. When, years later, I was trying to make sense of the work I had been doing, I found myself wondering how I would describe the moments of closeness with the child during these consultations. Challenging, pleasurable, puzzling, exciting, rewarding, and gratifying were the words that came to my mind. Challenging because I was presented with a problem and I wanted to try hard and discover the answer the child was searching for. Pleasurable because I enjoy chatting to a child who displays his capacity to explore ways of conveying some particular point to me. Puzzling and exciting because we were now a pair sifting through clues and seeking an elusive answer that we both wanted to find. Rewarding because few professional situations can be more gratifying than discovering something that will help someone who puts his trust in us. I could not quite see myself as having taken part in a sacred experience.

Somehow, Winnicott's word "sacred" seems to introduce a mystical element into this picture. I imagine that he wanted to convey the poetic beauty of a child at one with a giving object, rather than any religious implication. But this view of the encounter remains a highly individual one. I would assume that my own perception is a consequence of my personal experience of work as an area of my life where I offer the child (or another patient) my expertise, my professional ego. Winnicott's emphasis on the responsibility of the consultant to meet the child's trust and make sure the child is not disappointed appears to refer to personal attributes, almost something of an ideal to be aimed at and yet a goal that most practitioners might not be able to achieve. This is in line with comments I have heard about my work, where my "intuition" is seen as the main instrument I use to make contact with and understand the child. I find it difficult to accept that this should be so. Intuition is an important ingredient of our work, even if we call it "empathy" or attribute our understanding to experience or learning. But intuition alone would not enable the consultant to recognize the significance of the child's communications. I strongly believe that these consultations can be undertaken by most competent professionals, though there is no doubt that it is extremely difficult to formulate specific technical steps that should be followed. My impression is that most professionals feel daunted by the prospect of conversing with very young children; consequently, when they read or hear of a child's thinking expressed in the language of adults, they tend to marvel at the consultant's capacity to understand that child's language. As a matter of fact, this corresponds to situations where some parents will voice their admiration that I had "managed" to get their child to say things that they had never even considered the child would have thought or felt.

When I had colleagues observing consultations similar to those to be described in this book, I often heard the comment that they "had been listening and watching, trying to take everything in, but somehow feeling they were just floundering—suddenly, when I put the child's unconscious fantasy into words, it all fell into place and the whole picture just seemed terribly obvious". I believe that the problem lies in *how* one listens, how one processes all that the child says or expresses in words, play, or drawings. Once I am satisfied that I have a good picture of the child's emotional development, I concentrate on discovering the unconscious fantasy that I believe underlies the child's symptoms. There is a parallel with detective stories: some people are satisfied with the flow of events, while others are keen to spot the criminal before the author reveals who that was. In most assessment interviews, the consultant has an *a priori* idea of which treatment will be prescribed, and this is bound to influence the manner in which he addresses the child. I approach these diagnostic meetings with the objective of establishing the nature of the child's problem, and the issue of which treatment is required does not concern me at this point. I believe that the child wants to let me know how he experiences his problems, and I try, therefore, to decipher the child's cues and to figure out the message being conveyed to me.

I have found that as soon as the child feels that we *want to help and to understand* what bothers him, he will put forward the cues that can lead us to recognize the content of his fantasy. This is a process that escapes the child's conscious awareness, but there must be a subtle and elusive sequence of gradual revelations that depend on some feedback from the consultant for their unfolding. As I listen to the child, I am, obviously, interpreting his words against the background of my previous experience and my theoretical framework, but I am sure that many of my questions and comments are not correct or effective. I see the child as the one and only competent person to gauge my contributions, which means that I watch his reactions to decide whether I "have got it right" or whether I should think again and try harder. To repeat what I believe is the fundamental point here: I do not see the child "resisting", "denying", being hostile, or anything similar; rather, I am convinced that even if the child's explicit communications might suggest these interpretations, I see him as determined to enable me to find the way to unravelling the fantasy that causes him distress and pain. But, much as any observing colleague, for a great part of the interview I feel that I am floundering, trying to put data together, searching to identify missing bits of the jigsaw, to discover which questions might elicit the relevant information. The *dénoue-ment*, when I finally understand the fantasy I am looking for, varies from case to case, but it brings an incomparable sense of relief and the pleasure of completing a task. But next comes the challenge of working out *how* to convey this to the child.

Predictably, as soon as the last piece of the puzzle falls into place, it is possible to look back and recognize the clues that the child had put forward throughout the interview. This still means that the consultant has to be able to pick them up, even if not really grasping their significance. I have tried to emphasize my belief that the child will also sense what is expected of him during the interview, so that this becomes a joint venture where both child and consultant try to discover what lies in the child's unconscious. Winnicott's attitude to the child during his therapeutic consultations must have conveyed the degree of interest he had in what the child needed to express. It is the combination of these attitudes of child and consultant that Winnicott thought composed the "sacred" special ambience of his consultations. I suspect that what he later conceptualized as the "good-enough mother", the "facilitating environment", and the "use of the object" are reflections of that specific attitude of his to a child in a treatment context, particularly in the therapeutic consultations, when he offered himself to the child as an adult who wanted to hear, to know, to understand, and to help without intending to intrude or make claims on the child's feelings. These concepts have proved very valuable in our object-relations theories of child development, but, when taken as attributes required from a consultant if he is to undertake these interviews, it is possible that they might intimidate most young practitioners. My own experience has been that children will make considerable allowances for my mistakes and try very hard to help me find my way to the right question.

The older the child, the better equipped he will be to use words to engage with the consultant. The advantage of having play materials available is that they bring out more easily the unconscious contents of the child's conflicts and they do not arouse the same degree of defensiveness as words tend to do. But the consultant has to be prepared to mould himself to the child's choices of the means of communication. All being equal, I prefer to use drawings because they can be preserved and consulted again whenever necessary, but I will always accept the child's choice of which "language" to utilize during the interview.

Some adolescents will almost take offence if offered play material or drawings. I have, however, seen youngsters (and adults) who reached a point in their accounts where words escaped them or they found themselves describing some experience that they could not make sense of, usually because of some element that did not fit the whole story as they remembered it. In such a situation, I suggest to them that if they were able to put on paper the image they had in mind, they might find clues that escaped them when they were trying to express the specific experience or memory in words. Many youngsters will see the logic in this and proceed to draw the memory they are struggling with (see "Georgia", chapter four).

When I feel reasonably confident that the child has gone as far as he can in describing his situation in words, I suggest that he should "make a drawing for me". Most children are happy to do this, and, as they draw, I turn to the parents to ask them for their version of the situation. It is useful, though not always possible, to place the child in a position that allows us to have some view of the drawing he is making. If , however, the child cannot articulate his thoughts very easily and finds it equally difficult to cope with the blank page on which he might draw, then I try to engage him in a squiggle game. Some toys are available in the room, and the child may well decide, at some point, to play with these. Most children will ask the inevitable "What should I draw?", but they will always accept the evasive, "Oh, just anything you like, really . . .". Once I give the child the sheets of paper (always good-quality white paper, a detail that becomes important if one wants to make a copy of the picture drawn by the child) and a selection of pens, I try to ensure that the child decides how precisely he wants to use the drawing materials. Some children will finish one picture and immediately embark on a second, others will show their drawing to me or to the parents; however, quite often we find that children will only indicate having finished their drawing when there is a clear break in the discussion with the parents. Most children seem keen to pretend that they are not following the conversation in the room. Occasionally, they will chip in information, corrections, or other comments, but only seldom will they take the initiative to break into the discussion. In spite of the appearance of not paying attention to the conversation, I have found many cases where the drawing presents the child's version of the subjects being discussed with me by the parents. Such an occurrence gives particular poignancy to any divergence in the manner in which each of them experiences the events under discussion.

As the child concentrates on his drawing, the parents seem to feel that they now have "their turn", and it can be quite surprising to hear a parent voice some information which makes the child jump, claiming that this was the first time he had heard it. It is as if the parents had "forgotten" that the child could actually hear their words. This can be a difficult situation to deal with, but it always throws light on the patterns of interaction in the family.

The parents

In *Playing and Reality* (1971a), Winnicott describes some meetings with mothers in the presence of their young children. These accounts are more detailed than the references to mothers seen in his paediatric or child psychiatric clinics for consultations, and they show more clearly the warmth and care with which he addresses them. At the same time, he watches carefully the movements of their babies, and one can almost feel the closeness between Winnicott and the mother and her baby.

Mothers play a very important role in Winnicott's conceptualizations of child development; he will often speak of "parents" in his formulations, but, in fact, fathers do not appear much in descriptions of his clinical work. Winnicott is one of the few psychoanalytic theorists who gave great importance to the real, actual influence the parents have on the child, not only in earliest infancy, but throughout the child's life. In spite of this, the therapeutic consultations focus very specifically on the child alone, and the parents are not addressed as objects of Winnicott's assessment, except insofar as he evaluates their capacity to enable the child to build on the gains from the consultation.

I find it puzzling that Winnicott did not extend his diagnostic investigations to an assessment of the parents' psychopathology.

This choice might derive from his medical view of the child being "the patient", but it comes, more probably, from his psychoanalytic frame of reference. Here, it is acknowledged that the child is part of an environment, but it is the child's psyche that is the focus of study. The outside world will influence the child's experience of himself in the world, but it is the child's inborn psychological make-up that will determine how he interprets that input and formulates those images (representations) and ideas (fantasies) that constitute the child's view of himself and of the world in which he lives. Irrespective of how parents or other people treat the child, from a psychoanalytic perspective it is the child's unconscious fantasies that indicate what each of these people means to the child; this is what will help us to understand the rationale for the appearance and/or persistence of the symptoms that bring the child to us, and I suppose that this is what led Winnicott to concentrate his attention on the child himself.

Nevertheless, other workers saw the parents in different ways. Selma Fraiberg (1980) examined closely how parents treated their infants, and she put forward the concept of the "ghosts in the nursery", an inspired and colourful way of describing her finding of parents who saw their infants as a representation (a new version) of a person who had played a significant role in their earlier life. A major implication of her work is the extent to which the infant's behaviour will reflect the way in which he is treated—for example, a baby who cries incessantly but then stops when his mother discovers that she has been approaching him with the (unconscious) belief that he is doomed to become handicapped as was a younger brother of hers. It is easy enough to hypothesize that the baby is reacting to the anxiety that he senses in his mother, but it is still a remarkable finding to discover that his crying will only change or stop after the mother can treat him differently and that this, in its turn, only happens when she can recognize the source of her worries and accept that her baby is normal.

Fraiberg's work opened up the new field of infant psychiatry, and her approach to babies has been carried over by many other professionals to work with older children. The common denominator of these various techniques is not only the view that the child's symptoms originate in the parent(s)' way of treating him, but also the recognition that the parents can be a valuable source of help.

Whenever a child is discussed, many of his difficulties will sooner or later, implicitly or explicitly, be attributed to the pathological behaviour of one or both parents. What we now have come to recognize is that many parents, given the help they need, can change their approach to the child and become a very effective agent working for the improvement or cure of the child's problems. As the parent(s) perceive their child differently, they can alter the way in which they treat the child, and very quickly the child's "pathological behaviour" disappears. It is important, nevertheless, to consider whether the child also needs some help to understand the unconscious feelings and ideas that he has built in order to make sense of the parents' way of treating him.

In my own practice, I have found that there is much to be gained from having the parents present at the initial meeting with the child. Some parents prefer to see me before bringing the child, and I see no reason to refuse this. The most common excuse for such a preference is the parents' assertion that they have "certain things" that they would not like to discuss in front of the child. I often think that the objective is also to put me under the microscope, and I see this as a perfectly legitimate step and am happy to concur, but I still make explicit my preference for a first meeting including the child. The explanation I offer parents to justify this request is the fact that child and parents would then all know how the problems are presented, and we can always decide in the course of the meeting how and when to split up the participants. Whatever is decided, I make a note that the issue of privacy/ sharing may be an important element in the family dynamics.

The main reason for my wanting the parents present at the first interview with the child is that I have found that many parents have little idea of the child's actual experience of his problems and of life in general. "I never knew that this is how he felt . . ." is a comment that I have heard more times than I would ever have guessed it was possible. We tend to assume that, because they live together, parents and children would have a pool of shared experiences and that parents would therefore have some notion of what the child feels about people and events in their home life, if not in other areas of his life. On the whole, we consider that "family life" implies some degree of *discussion* of each other's experiences and sentiments. If we think of difficulties experienced by some member of the family, again we might want to think that the family living together would not allow for much isolation. Working with children, time and again we discover that in practice whenever the child displays his difficulty/problem/symptom, immediately this leads the parents to implement their idea of what would make that problem disappear. Sadly, even when there is love and goodwill, there is only limited capacity to elicit the child's own perception of his experience. As a rule, parents will promptly get hold of what they consider the normal or reasonable manner in which the child *should* be experiencing the situation and proceed to advise him accordingly. When this happens, perhaps predictably the child experiences the parents (or parent) not as allies who try to understand his feelings, but as people who expect him to feel and behave in line with their own views—and this can often put the parents as fitting in precisely with the dreaded image that is part of the child's unconscious fantasied meaning of the problem. This leads to the persistence of the symptoms, which inevitably makes it so that the parents continue to search for a new way through which they can make the child adopt their views. I believe that only such a pattern can explain the surprise that so many parents indicate when in the course of our joint meeting they hear the child's explanation of how he experiences his difficulties and realize that they had never considered that the child might actually have thoughts different from their own previous perception of the situation.

For many children, the consultation seems to offer the opportunity of "opening up"; perhaps this is due to feeling protected by the presence of a stranger, but it is also possible that this might be the first time when someone actually *asked* for their account. Having the parents in the room allows the consultant a first-hand opportunity of discovering how each parent reacts to their child's statements. If some parents react with surprise and a clear sense of regret and shame at not having elicited those statements from the child themselves, others will ignore the child's words, others will correct their accounts, others still will not pay so much attention to the words as focus on the child's attitude "when speaking to the doctor"—the variations are endless, but these are live situations that allow us to have some idea of how child and parents relate to each other in their ordinary life. Some parents might justify correcting the child as resulting from the need to give the consultant a "truthful" account of events or from the wish to remind the child that he must be at his best behaviour at all times. However plausible and/or acceptable these explanations might appear, it is important to note that these attitudes may still indicate the possibility that these are parents who cannot see the child as a separate individual with feelings of his own and expect, therefore, that the child must behave and speak at all times in line with the parents' view of a situation. If confirmed by further findings, this interpretation will lead us to plan our therapeutic intervention with full awareness of the parents' difficulty in allowing the child his own private experience of the world.

As mentioned earlier, I always try to engage the child first at the beginning of the consultation, and most parents are happy to sit back and wait. After a while, when I feel reasonably clear about the child's view of the problems and of his life at home, school, and so on, I will ask the parents to give me some idea of *who they are*. All parents laugh at such a question, and they want me to specify what precisely I want to know. I explain that I would like to have a framework against which to appreciate the child's story, adding that perhaps they could give me an idea of their families of origin, their education, their work, how they met, and how they came to be in their present position. Some parents take this question as an intrusion into their privacy, and some also justify this view by pointing out that it is their child who needs help, but, even then, most parents feel that this is intellectually acceptable and proceed to tell me of what they believe is relevant. I take it that it is my task to decide when I should ask supplementary questions in order to obtain a clearer view of some detail of the history of each parent as an individual and an understanding of how they experience the development of their marital life and the eventual arrival of the child(ren). Occasionally, a parent will question the relevance of these questions. I try to explain that because their child grew up in their company, their personal history, customs, beliefs, could all be relevant for me to understand their child. If they are not convinced, I will some times ask how they would explain the fact that their child speaks English rather than some other language. This sounds a rather silly question, but it does make the point that a child's development is influenced by how their parents live and what they teach him, explicitly or implicitly.

I process the parents' accounts on three levels: (1) the factual data that have marked each person's progress in life, (2) the explicit and implicit feelings towards significant people in their past and present lives, and (3) any possible links with the child's presenting symptoms. From a consideration of these levels, I hope to reach some hypotheses about each parent's experience of the child and his problems, about the other parent, and, last but not least, about their feelings concerning seeing me and what they hope to obtain from me.

Some children struggle with difficulties that require more help than any parent might give them, and in such a situation we have to try to help the parents to understand and accept the limits of what they can do for their child. It is safe to assume that when a child is referred to a child psychiatrist or analyst for an assessment, his parents believe that their child's problems result from not only individual, but also family pathology—this can be expressed by the classical "I know it's my fault, but . . .", through a whole gamut of variations, leading to a sensible "Perhaps there is something which I am not doing right?" If we then find that the child's symptoms derive from some organic pathology, this should be discussed in detail with the parents. Clearly, whatever non-dynamic manifestations the child displays, by the time he comes to see us a complex range of reactive, adaptive behaviours will have been developed by both child and parents. But the consultant has the responsibility of disentangling (or, at least, of trying to disentangle) what can be changed in the child's symptoms and what is part of pathology which requires some other medical or psychological intervention (see "Paula", chapter five; see also "David", in Brafman, 1997, pp. 776–777). By far the most painful cases are those where parents demonstrate a sense of guilt for "causing the child's problems" when, in fact, this is an unconscious defence against a sense of helplessness caused by pathology in the child that is beyond their wish to help him.

The fact that, apart from his presenting complaints, a child has made age-appropriate progress in the various stages of his development by the time the family comes to see us indicates not only the child's normal endowment, but also the parents' capacity to help him reach those earlier milestones. I see this as a fundamental implication of our object-relation theories—that is, for a child to gain independence from the parents, he needs not only a normal psychological endowment, but also parents who can tolerate the child moving away from them. The child's presenting symptoms will, therefore, point to a possible obstacle that the parents cannot overcome because of some unconscious factor of their own: we could use Winnicott's word "knot" to describe this situation. A "knot" indicates an impediment, an obstacle occurring against the background of normal development, and this is why Winnicott stressed that, once this knot was cleared up, the child was free to resume his normal growth process. Though Winnicott used this word referring to the child, I find it also a useful description of a similar specific blockage in one or both parents' parenting functions. For the sake of brevity, we can say that child and parents have become caught in a "knot".

Surprising as it may seem, it is usually not difficult to find an explanation as to why parents have been unable to help the child to overcome his problem. It is quite possible that parents come to the initial consultation with the same charge of hope/expectation of obtaining help that Winnicott described in the children he saw. I have met parents who disclosed quite intimate experiences at these initial joint interviews, and I had to assume that they were responding to an internal need of their own as much as to a climate in the meeting that made them feel that help might be available.

Not all parents are able and/or willing to engage in these investigations. Some refuse to attend, others decline to answer questions, and some request to be seen privately. Considering that the explicit aim of the consultation is to find help for the child (i.e. not for the parent), I accept whatever decision a parent makes, but this has to be noted as a datum to be considered when trying to establish the best way of helping the child. In other words, I do not have an *a priori* view that the child's problems *are* or *are not* part of the dynamics of their family life: I see the initial consultation as an exploration of normal and abnormal areas of the functioning of the personality of each participant, with particular attention paid to how each member of the family affects the others. Each case we see is bound to present features resulting from the obvious fact that child and parents live together, but we have to evaluate the relevance of each finding. The vast majority of cases that come our way will not allow a definite elucidation of what is *cause* and what is *effect*, but we have to hold an open mind to the possibility that some of our patients present pathological pictures that require attention in their own right. If it becomes clear that the child or one or both parents need help as individuals, this will require careful attention. It can prove very difficult, for technical or even ethical considerations, to establish that there is individual non-dynamic pathology in one of the family members, but this still does not eliminate the problem that holding an interview that utilizes a dynamic framework will always carry the implication that we believe this to be the approach of choice for the problem that we are proposing to treat. When it is the child who requires another approach, this is usually not difficult to handle. (For example, a 15-year-old girl was referred with a presumed diagnosis of anorexia nervosa, since she had low body weight and eating difficulties, together with complex problems in her relationship with her mother; finding that she had never menstruated, I requested a check-up, and she was found to have severe atresia of her genital organs.) However, problems are more delicate when it is a parent who requires investigation.

When a child's presenting problem is recognized to be an intrinsic part of a parent's conflicts, this can be easily dealt with when the relevant parent can accept coming for help in his own right. (For example, an 11-year-old boy—"Gamal", in Brafman, 1999—was referred with aural hallucinations, and our discussion pinpointed how these were more intense and more prolonged when he was with his mother. As she recognized that earlier experiences had produced intense fears and worries over her son's emotional development, this mother embarked on individual therapy—and the son's hallucinations disappeared before long.)

Besides allowing for a more comprehensive diagnostic evaluation of a child's problems, an important advantage of the approach presented here is the opportunity given to the parents to be the effective helpers of their child. Some (few!) families seem to perceive the benefits of the techniques employed in the joint consultation and carry over into their daily life its style of asking questions to their children, rather than indicating what answer they expect to hear from them. A second group of parents sees these meetings as no more than an unavoidable therapeutic intervention, but, if they continue life "as before", they still manage to change their approach to the referred child and help him to overcome his symptoms. Sadly, there is a third group of parents who simply dismiss the whole idea of having a *verbal interchange* with the child. It is easy enough to explain the attitude of parents in this group by arguing that this is a matter of culture—that is, upbringing plus a mix of social mores and personality factors. But, however difficult, for diagnostic and prognostic purposes it is important to try to differentiate whether this stance results (1) from a particular preconceived idea of what a child is or (2) from an emotional incapacity to grant the child the status of a separate individual, with his own (developmentally appropriate) needs, thoughts, and feelings. Parents in one of these two types may present as if they belonged to the other type; indeed, the types are not mutually exclusive but they still constitute two different categories, each of which carries its own prognostic implications—prejudices may be open to change, but the capacity to distinguish between self and object does not tend to respond to therapeutic inputs.

I have always been puzzled by hearing parents praise me for getting their child to voice thoughts and feelings they had not even suspected he might hold and yet, at the same time, appear convinced that the child would never behave in a similar fashion within the family setting. Many parents rationalize their belief that they could not duplicate my "feat" by attributing it to my being a psychoanalyst or to my age, but I am inclined to believe that the crucial element here is the attitude held towards the child. A simple way of exploring what lies behind such assertions is to ask parents at which age they believe children begin to think for themselves: the answers will vary enormously and will give us significant pointers to understanding the parents' feelings. The concept of the child as an individual is theoretically reasonably clear, and people feel quite comfortable arguing over "the rights of the child", though often enough some of these activists know more about the conceptual child than about real, individual, children. Nevertheless, it is a fact that different cultures and social classes attribute varying values and abilities to the child at each age. However fascinating these issues are from a philosophical, social, and psychological point of view, we must, when focusing on a specific family, besides considerations of class, social status, religion, cultural, social, and educational background, also pay careful attention to the theory of object relations and assess the level at which each parent can relate to his or her spouse and his or her child.

This evaluation can help us to understand the difficulty that some parents have in grasping our offering them a view of their child that clashes with the one they have held. In extreme cases, it does not seem to matter that the child voices a view that diverges from the one that the parent holds, since that parent sincerely believes he knows both how the child feels and what he thinks. When we meet parents who cannot change the picture they hold of their child, it is fruitless to plan helping programmes that depend on their active involvement. But quite often we find parents who are unable to consider changing their view of the child and, yet, will agree to cooperate with the child's embarking on individual therapy. This must always be welcome and efforts be made to find such treatment, since this kind of cooperation may stem from a genuine wish that somebody else helps the child—I sometimes speak of a "Miriam's syndrome", thinking of the biblical Miriam who ensured that her brother Moses obtained elsewhere the upbringing he needed. We only need to worry when this apparent acquiescence comes from an ambivalent attitude to the child and a false attempt to impress the professional: these children are never allowed to stay long in treatment. Clearly, this is a difficult diagnostic challenge, but one that must be seriously considered.

The consultation

It is very rare that children should be referred for a one-off interview. Occasionally, a child will come from far away and it is known that further attendances will be difficult, if not impossible, but the vast majority of referrals do not impose a time limit to the consultant's work. A referral is, by definition, a statement that the referrer finds himself unable to help that child and that he believes that we might be able to achieve this. Most referrals will, explicitly or implicitly, assume that we will provide the kind of help that the referrer believes we tend to offer. This is part of the usual dynamics of referrals, where specialists are seldom seen as operating within a broad spectrum of alternatives—instead, there is something of a prescription already contained in the choice of specialist. This makes it particularly important that the specialist should feel free to prescribe what he (and not the referrer) thinks the client needs. It is sometimes well worth considering making it explicit to the patients that the consultant is setting out to *assess* the client's needs—that is, the consultant is allowing himself *carte blanche* to conduct his investigations with no definite commitment to carry this over into a specific therapy.

It is probably a result of medical tradition that a diagnostic assessment will usually be seen as occupying an extended single visit (between 1½ and 2 hours). At one point, some analysts practised assessments that were called "trial analyses", which could extend over several weeks, if not months. However, these were not diagnostic evaluations *sensu strictu*, as much as attempts to establish whether the patient was suitable for psychoanalysis. Nowadays, in the world of psychotherapy, assessments have become spread out over a few interviews, and there is a considerable literature discussing the differences between therapy and assessment, though many authors question the validity of such an argument. This issue will not be discussed here in any detail, but the present context demands a definition of what constitutes a "consultation".

Winnicott's approach (and language) is essentially medical, and the cases to be described in subsequent chapters follow the same model. Winnicott thought and conceptualized his findings within a psychoanalytic framework, but he followed the doctor's basic duty *vis-à-vis* his patients: they came for help, and his goal was to do his best to relieve their suffering. Some readers may find this a curious, redundant statement, but already in Winnicott's days we had many analysts who argued that we should not define our contract with the patient as proposing to *treat* him. Instead, they chose the formulation that analysts would try to help the patient to *understand* the meaning of his symptoms, thoughts, and feelings—a quaint way of conveying to the patient that they saw psychoanalysis as an instrument of *research* and not necessarily as a treatment. As is well known, "psychoanalysis" is considered to denote three different disciplines: a method of therapy, a system of psychology, and an instrument of investigation—but if this is a valid theoretical conceptualization, once a professional charges fees to a client who is seeking help for his problems, there is no logical way of avoiding the interpretation that the practitioner is, at least implicitly, proposing to deliver some kind of healing that is meant to help the patient.

When first meeting the child, Winnicott was the diagnostician—a doctor trying to identify the illness, the cause, for the patient's suffering. The finding that the interview could produce therapeutic effects came *after* the diagnostic evaluation of the child and his family. Embarking on an initial interview with a mind-set that this will be a one-off therapeutic consultation would constitute an incorrect understanding of Winnicott's work and, furthermore, might also lead the consultant to miss important data.

Many of the children described in *Therapeutic Consultations* (Winnicott, 1971b) were seen in a child psychiatric clinic, but child psychiatrists virtually ignored the book. The book was seen to bypass the issue of psychiatric diagnoses, and it discussed issues not seen to belong to the world of psychiatry. Psychoanalysts also took a critical stance: Winnicott was valuing immediate results at the probable cost of allowing the children's "deeper problems" to remain unattended to. Virtually no reference to this work is found in the psychoanalytic literature. Only the squiggle game has gained a life of its own, as child psychotherapists and also some other professionals who work with children have adopted it. As often happens with some discoveries, the original context of therapeutic consultations has been left behind, and the squiggles are now seen as a useful technique of establishing contact with young patients.

Over the years, more analysts have applied psychoanalytic concepts to other settings and developed new theories and techniques, thereby widening the scope of clinical interventions. Infant psychiatry has been mentioned earlier, but "brief psychotherapy", "focal therapy", and "family therapy" are some of the offshoots deriving from the application of psychodynamic concepts to specific settings, with varying goals, but with the common denominator of being therapies that do not demand the years of treatment that psychoanalysis stands for. As mentioned earlier, Winnicott himself discussed the difference between psychoanalytic treatment and his therapeutic consultations, and he put forward the idea of doing "as much as possible" as compared to doing "as much as necessary". This might suggest the influence of what one could call "pragmatic reality", but this interpretation opens the door to a suspicion of short-changing clients, somehow not doing justice to their needs. Such arguments have the quality of partisan disputes, where what is at stake is the validity of particular therapeutic techniques. This tends to cloud over the fundamental question of what is, in fact, the patient's problem and what treatment is best suited to his needs.

From my point of view, I believe that the most important element of this discussion is the fact that *when first seeing the young patient*, whatever his age, we must consider that encounter a *diagnostic* interview. The objective is to identify (diagnose) the child's problem and then consider how best to meet *his* needs. Analysis or therapy, long-term or short-term, intensive or less frequent sessions, individual or family meetings, male or female therapist/analyst—there is little hope that any two professionals will agree on the recommendation they will make to a particular patient. For better or for worse, in practice it is one's own criteria that will determine the diagnosis, prognosis, and prescription given to the patient. This means that it is vitally important that each practitioner is very clear about the principles that guide his work.

I imagine most, if not all, readers will agree with the above definition of a consultation. It is more difficult to pinpoint how and when the diagnostic assessment moves on to become a therapeutic intervention, but this is a task that must be attempted.

The therapeutic consultation

Most children are referred for help with a specific complaint, such as enuresis, restlessness, nightmares, and so forth. A small proportion of children are recognized by parents or a physician to present diffuse problems suggestive of some developmental condition. With practice, one discovers that "the reason" why parents take their child to a medical practitioner seems to depend more on the parents' view of what constitutes tolerable behaviour than on the specific problem presented by the child. Bedwetting is a prime example of this phenomenon: the age at which the child is referred to the child psychiatrist or psychologist (or, for that matter, to the urologist) seems to depend entirely on the views held by parents and doctors—it is only very rarely that any of them will consider the issue of the child's self-esteem. Speech difficulties are another example of this curious mixture of knowledge and preconceived ideas, leading to some children receiving no help for many years.

Each time we read a referral letter, we build an image of the child in question, but it is only rarely that we meet the "real child" and find that our imaginary picture fits the reality we now see in front of us. This is because many GPs and paediatricians tend to take the parents' account as an accurate picture of the child, when in fact the parents' image of the child is very influenced by their own personal experiences. A dramatic example of this is the case of "Jane", aged 8 years, which is reported in chapter three: the mother reported that Jane suffered severe headaches, and the GP referred the child to the paediatrician to assess the possibility of some migraine variation. Talking to the girl, it emerged that, from her own point of view, her worst suffering was caused by her bedwetting. Her mother was surprised to hear of this since she believed that this problem had long been overcome, but she promptly went on to dismiss its significance because she herself had wet the bed until aged 10 years.

Meeting the child makes it possible for the consultant to establish how the child has conveyed his problems to the parents and how each of these interpreted what they heard and saw. As described earlier, depending on the child's age we have to employ various techniques that help us to explore those areas of the child's experience that might enable us to assess how the child is negotiating his developmental milestones and dealing with the challenges produced by life in the family, school, neighbourhood, and so forth. It is in the course of this investigation that we can establish how circumscribed or diffuse are the child's difficulties, as well as how accurate is the parents' account of how they see the child. We can find a child like "David" (see Brafman, 1997, pp. 776–77) who is referred because of severe nightmares and then turns out to have a cognitive handicap, much as the child referred for aural hallucinations ("Gamal", see Brafman, 1999, pp. 350–352) who is then found to be suffering from a reactive anxiety state. David had never been able to let his parents know the contents of his nightmares, something that might conceivably have led them to stop the boy from watching horror films; the other boy's mother reacted with immense anxiety to her son's account of "hearing voices" because of having seen cases of psychotic breakdown earlier in her life.

It is through careful and detailed questioning of the child that we can gradually build an image of the precise nature of the child's pathology and how this is interwoven with the parents' perception of the child's problems. As the interview moves on, hypotheses are continuously being built in the consultant's mind as to how the child's account in the interview links up with what the child has communicated to his parents about his difficulties—and how each parent's interpretation of the child's difficulties influences the way they treat the child. Each hypothesis leads to a different line of inquiry, and it is only slowly and very gradually that a clearer view is reached of what lies behind the child's presenting symptom. If this is the "tip of the iceberg"—that is, an acute crisis built on a baseline of a more serious problem—this points to the necessity of instituting specialized, long-term help; if one or both parents have problems that require more detailed attention, then this is the direction to be followed. If, however, it is established that the child and the parents have worked successfully together in most areas of the child's development, but now the child has become stuck in a "knot"—a vicious circle where the child's and the parents' anxieties are keeping in place a pathological situation—then the possibility looms large that a therapeutic intervention might occur within the context of that originally diagnostic meeting.

Unravelling the content of the child's unconscious fantasy that created and/or sustains his symptoms enables us to find ways of conveying this to the child. There is something extremely poignant in a child's expression when discovering what has been haunting him and has been creating pain and distress. They show their sense of relief and pleasure in quite visible, dramatic manner. Sometimes, the parents react to the consultant's words as if they were utmost nonsense, but some children are able to confirm that the interpretation is correct—most parents will then show the curious expression of someone whose intelligence clamours against accepting the consultant's interpretation, while their love for the child forces them to recognize that, somehow, the child has welcomed what they all heard.

As described earlier, the child seems to come to the consultation with a kind of preparedness to convey those data that may help the consultant to recognize the content of the unconscious idea that sustains the presence of the child's symptoms. Whether the child is engaged in words alone or in play or in drawings depends on the personal preference of each consultant and the response of each child. But if it is the unconscious fantasy that is being searched, this will become recognizable in most cases. The actual phrasing of this understanding has to be gauged taking into account the age of the child, but it is usually not difficult to find the right words to express this interpretation. I firmly believe that at this point the child is ready to "give up" his symptom, but in practice I have found that the parents' attitude towards the child is the decisive factor as to whether real change occurs or, instead, the problem persists. Here lies the need to search for the nature of each parent's input to the situation. Given enough information, we can identify the factors that lead each parent to treat the child in a manner that perpetuates the symptom: if they can accept our interpretation of what motivates their "misperception" of the child and, accordingly, change their approach to the child, then real change in their interaction occurs and, of course, the presenting symptom(s) disappears.

Whatever the outcome of this initial interview, I will always offer the family a follow-up appointment. This gives us the opportunity to discuss any doubts that were left from the first meeting or to take up any issues that have arisen over the interval. This session should also focus on prognosis. It is obviously difficult to predict how lasting any improvement will be, but the issue must not be avoided. Above all, I like to get across to the child and to the parents that I would always be available for any further discussions. If I believe the child could benefit from long-term therapy, I make this clear and I explain the reasons why I think this should be undertaken immediately or whether it should be thought of as a possibility to be considered at a later date. A rather delicate complication can occur when parents feel that their new approach to the child has led to the child's improvement—in such a situation, the recommendation for individual therapy can be taken as a statement of mistrust in their capacity to help the child, and it is important not to undermine their self-confidence. If we still believe the child does need the long-term therapeutic input, it is best to opt for the compromise of organizing a series of follow-up appointments, which will allow us to observe how the situation develops.

The drawings

It will be seen in the cases that follow that I make considerable use of drawings when trying to the elucidate the child's unconscious fantasy. Children will speak to me and answer my questions because they have learnt that this is part of meeting a stranger, particularly a doctor, but they also know that they have to be careful with what they say, because they cannot guess how their words will be interpreted. Drawing, on the other hand, is usually seen as fun, as play, an activity that most (not all) children will engage in without feeling uneasy or threatened. Some children will react with near panic when confronting an empty sheet of paper, but most of these will manage to engage in a game of squiggles. Occasionally, a child will say "I cannot really draw . . .", but they tend to accept the explanation that they are not under scrutiny, that there is no intention of giving them marks or judging the quality of whatever they put on paper.

As mentioned earlier, I have found that drawings will convey thoughts and feelings that the child might not be able to put into words—not just out of anxiety, but also because their unconscious perception of some situation might not have formed itself in words. Obviously, this is a hypothesis that I cannot prove, but the expression of illumination and discovery—never of surprise—I have seen on the faces of some children when they hear the words that purport to articulate an unconscious thought of theirs suggests that they can recognize how familiar is the idea expressed by me, as though it is a revelation of something they had known all along.

The squiggle game itself is discussed in detail in the next section. However, my interpretation of isolated drawings might require some comments. It will be seen that I do not consider the pictures as indications of conflicts linked to the child's instinctual developmental phases (e.g. phallic or anal elements). It is conceivable that this might prove instructive, but I choose to think of the drawings as a language that the child utilizes to convey his thoughts and feelings. I take them as alternative communication data that complement the child's conversation and clarify any gaps left in the verbal account. In chapter three, Figure 3.5 exemplifies these alternative interpretations: I chose to interpret the child's feelings that her outside, social appearance did not correspond to the pain, the real turmoil that was hidden underneath. I have found colleagues who would have interpreted, instead, the oral, cannibalistic impulses that the child was representing with the voracious fish, feelings that originated in her hostile resentment towards her mother. In chapter five, Figure 5.8 might be taken as a pointer to phallic rivalry conflicts between the boy and his father, but because of the total context of the story I chose to interpret the boy's fears that his father might suffer a fatal accident in the course of his work. Perhaps the two interpretations are not mutually exclusive, in that one might be described as the conceptualization of one's findings and the other the actual clinical, explicit interpretation that is given to the patient. However, at the end of the day, it remains a matter of personal style as to which technique is chosen by each consultant.

The notion that the child might have an unconscious pictorial representation of some experience that cannot be translated into words helps me to make sense of cases I have found where the superimposition of two drawings reveals a meaning that would not be gathered from examining the two pictures separately. The cases of Georgia (chapter four) and Paula (chapter five) can be seen to present what I describe as "superimposed images". I have been asked about statistical validation of such a finding, which might eliminate the possibility of a simple coincidence. At one point, I did set out to search for this, visiting art colleges and asking volunteers to make drawings of any kind and in any number, provided that they made at least two pictures. When collecting the pictures, I asked each student what they had represented in their drawings and I wrote this down. Later, looking through the material, I discovered several examples of drawings that, when superimposed, brought out what I thought would be meanings that did not correspond to the stories I had been told. Clearly, it would be impossible to approach any of these students and ask for further clarification, since if one superimposition was "interesting", another suggested what I thought were suicidal thoughts.

I hope some colleague will investigate whether my findings are simply accidental or whether there is some other explanation for them. I feel confident in my belief that my own explanation is valid, since this splitting up of a "message" into two or more separate pieces that, when joined together, help us understand an unconscious thought is now well accepted when discussing spoken language. I believe that these are children who have some neurological ability to form images, which can then be represented in various different ways. In terms of pictures, the sheet of paper would represent some kind of frame equivalent to the mental image itself, which would explain the manner in which the two separate drawings complement each other when put together. Again, I must hope that a neuropsychologist colleague will substantiate my clinical finding.

Whether my interpretation of these pictures is "scientifically valid" or not, in each single case the child could immediately recognize what they had put on paper. In practice, when I suspect that the superimposition of pictures might bring out an "unintended" meaning, I explain to the child that I would like to put the two sheets of paper precisely on top of each other, matching each corner of both sheets, as if pretending that the two pictures were actually only one. Having put the two sheets on each other, I hold them against some source of light and ask the child if he sees anything there that looks new or different. Virtually every one smiles with some kind of embarrassment, as if they suddenly see something they recognize as theirs, even if they had not intended to display it.

Squiggles

To judge from the available literature, very few analysts or therapists have used the squiggle game as part of therapeutic consultations, along the lines described by Winnicott. Gampel (1995) uses the squiggle game in ordinary sessions of an ongoing therapy. She uses squiggle drawings in the same manner that another analyst or therapist would utilize spontaneous pictures drawn by the child in the course of a therapy session. Acciolly Lins (1990) employed the game in consultations with disadvantaged children in Brazil, as part of a doctoral thesis on Winnicott's work. The squiggles are seen as a technique to facilitate communication with children who might find it difficult to articulate their feelings, besides making it possible to obtain closer contact with the child within a limited space of time. Farhi (1996) refers to the squiggle game in a metaphorical way to describe the behaviour of an adult patient during her long-term psychotherapy. She writes of the complex pattern of interaction where the patient oscillates between opposing urges to reveal conflicts to the therapist and defences against this impulse.

Caldwell (personal communication 1970) and Hood (personal communication 1998), who worked with Winnicott in his child psychiatric clinic, employed the squiggle game as part of the diagnostic assessment of their patients, and it is quite possible that other child analysts and child psychiatrists have done the same. Considering the number of professionals who know and admire the squiggle game and its application in therapeutic consultations, it is quite puzzling that more papers have not been published on its use. On the other hand, the game has attracted objections of several kinds:

1. The analyst is seen as taking too active a part in the interaction with the child during the interview. Some of the analysts who raise this objection belong to that group of professionals who advocate the "analyst-as-a-mirror" stance in any kind of clinical encounter: the patient is not asked questions or given directives in any manner, under the rationale that this "neutral" posture would lead the patient to expose his problems and react to the analyst without any overt, explicit stimulus coming from the analyst. But some other analysts who feel free to formulate questions they consider relevant also object to the use of the squiggle game. They can accept that, by definition, the squiggle is *meant* not to convey a specific meaning; but whatever the child makes of these lines of the consultant is logically a response to a stimulus that, consciously or unconsciously, the consultant has offered to the child. How would the consultant respond if the child were to ask, explicitly, whether the consultant meant to draw that which the child perceives in the draw-

ing? The consultant may evade the question by some such phrasing as, "Well . . . if you think so, then perhaps it may well be the case . . .", but it may be far more difficult to deal with the question if the child has perceived something that the analyst definitely would not like to see in his lines. This is part of the argument that when the analyst restricts himself to words, he can at least find it easier to sort out any misunderstandings that may result from the child attributing to these words a meaning that does not match what the consultant wishes to express.

2. Not every professional trusts himself to be able to use pen or pencil to make drawings. Winnicott was a very competent artist, and his drawings are of sufficiently high quality to explain how he trusted himself to play the squiggle game with a child. Some artists claim that "anybody" can draw and that only inhibitions (what we call defences, leading to repression and anxiety related to the fear of self-exposure) lead us to avoid putting pen to paper in a spontaneous, un-self-conscious way. Whether this is true or not, it makes sense that professionals should prefer to try to implement in their work those conditions that enable them to function at their best and if drawing makes them feel ill at ease, then it is right that they should prefer not to engage in it. This would be an analyst who says, "Playing squiggles may be positive and effective, but it is not for me!"

3. A further criticism is implicit in point (1): with the drawings the consultant makes from the child's squiggles, the consultant is giving away something of his own psyche, and this is held by some to be wrong, whether the child can consciously recognize the content of the consultant's communication or not. A fashionable way of arguing against this criticism would be for the consultant to assert that his drawing is part of the countertransference to the child's unconscious conflicts, but I wonder whether Winnicott would ever agree that this was the case. However competent and experienced the consultant may be in keeping his observing functions under control during the interview, the flow of the consultation is bound to involve the analyst's unconscious in the sequence of pictures being made; it would follow that it can be difficult to establish the precise extent to which the analyst's drawings reflect (a) his counter-

transference, (b) his analytic scrutiny of the child's material, or (c) his own private psychopathology.

From my own experience, I find that my drawings are strongly influenced by the various interpretations I make of each of the child's drawings, as seen in the context of the child's verbal account: this represents a clear "contamination" of my supposed spontaneity. It happens, however, that drawing comes difficult to me, and I am always aware of my struggle to find some meaningful shape that might develop from the child's squiggle. The extent to which my "discovery" of something to put on paper stems from my ongoing reactions to the child's communications or from my own psychopathology may well be an important theoretical issue. Nonetheless, I have always been left with the impression that the child's drawings seem to follow a sequence dictated by the unconscious fantasy that he brings to the session. Furthermore, I do not really believe that the consultant's drawings carry a significance that can be compared to that of the child's creations, nor have I found any evidence to suggest that my squiggles or my drawings do influence those of the child. The precise origin of each squiggle and picture drawn by the consultant may well be a topic for discussion, but, as stated above, I am not sure that this can be established with any certainty. It would be a mistake, however, to pretend that this problem does not exist and to short-circuit it by arguing that the consultant's drawings stem from his countertransference to the child.

At the end of the day, even if children tend not to challenge the consultant as to why the consultant drew whatever it is he claims to have drawn, it is still possible that the child is influenced by that drawing. Critics could, therefore, be correct in claiming that the consultant's drawings affect the child. But, then, if we use logic quite strictly, the same argument must apply to the analyst's words and behaviour. The only way of dealing with this "danger" is that the analyst must be aware of what he offers the child (or any other patients)—this is the only way in which the analyst can gauge the content and nature of the child's response.

4.   It might be worth repeating, more succinctly, what is described in points (1) and (3): the squiggle game is a particularly tangible,

visible example of a consultant's contribution to his interaction with the child patient. If some will say that this game *influences* the flow of the child's communications, I would say, "Perhaps yes, but not necessarily negatively". Considering all cases where I have used squiggles, I believe that they have almost always *enabled* the child to express his unconscious—and I see this as very positive. But do we, in any case, really know any way in which a consultant can fail to influence his patient?

I have no doubt that we always influence our patients. A correct, timely, properly phrased and delivered interpretation will influence the patient just as much as some other verbal or behavioural contribution that the patient (consciously or unconsciously) objects to—or, for that matter, approves or likes. On the whole, we tend to consider our involvement in the interaction with the patient as a given, something we want to take for granted, and we tend to concentrate on the patient's side of the interaction. If the patient questions something that we did or said, more often than not this will be taken as an example of *the patient's* style of relating to another person. There is disagreement as to how the analyst should deal with his patient's objection to something that he did or said. Some analysts will accept a discussion of their contribution, while others will limit themselves to analysing the patient's feelings and statements. Whichever technical approach is chosen, we must hope that after the patient is gone, we should reassess our work on our own or with a colleague, so as to understand what happened during the interview. However, this applies to the therapist's words and attitudes as much as it applies to his playing the squiggle game: this "game" is only one other, certainly more exposed, example of how we influence the patients we see. Against any such objections, we should not forget that the squiggle game constitutes a very valuable tool to establish emotional contact with those children who experience difficulties with expressing themselves in words or who cannot engage in play or spontaneous drawings.

I feel comfortable engaging a child in the squiggle game when I am conducting a consultation, but I do not see it as a technique that I would use in the course of long-term therapy, since I cannot draw so easily and, anyway, the repetition of the game makes me suspicious of the dynamics underlying it. Many children, especially

latency-age ones, have a tendency to embark on repetitive activities, and I would consider it counterproductive for the therapist to
encourage or collude with the child's turning the game into what
could become a defensive, probably gratifying type of pseudo-
closeness. If long-term therapy enters a phase where a child is
silent or if we are working with a mute child, drawings can become
a valuable means of contact, but it is best to opt for "ordinary",
spontaneous drawings made by the child on his own.

The squiggle game is *one of many* techniques that can be employed to make contact with a child. I see the first interview as,
fundamentally, a diagnostic—that is, fact-finding—procedure, and
the initial challenge lies in establishing meaningful emotional contact with the child (or a patient of whatever age). Depending on the
child's age, I will first attempt to engage him with words. If the
child chooses to play with one of the toys that are available in the
room, I will follow him in this, trying to find links between my
questions and the child's play. I begin by asking the usual questions children assume all adults will ask when they first meet: how
does he feel?, friends?, school?, home?, siblings? Most, if not all,
children will allow us some latitude in our questions and give us
pointers to which subject they find acceptable as a beginning to a
conversation. Gradually, we can move to how the child experiences his problems.

After hearing the child's account of his problems and his life, I
usually ask him to make a drawing. Most children feel quite comfortable drawing, and I have found this a medium through which
a child (or an adult) can often express feelings, thoughts, and experiences that are not linked to words they recognize consciously.
But if a child is not particularly articulate, does not speak English
fluently, and/or is incapable of making a spontaneous drawing,
I turn to the squiggle game, where we can establish contact with
a minimum of words. It is very rare to find a child who refuses to
play squiggles.

If I am correct in my assumption that Winnicott engaged the
child in the squiggle game as a procedure of choice in his consultations, then my use of the game departs from that. My opting for
the sequence of alternatives I have described above follows from
finding that most children will express their unconscious conflicts
during that first diagnostic encounter—not only through squig-

gles, but in whatever happens to be their preferred mode of communication. The two main factors involved in what comes to be the channel of communication between consultant and child are (1) the child's capacity to convey his ideas in words, drawings, and/or play and (2) the consultant's personal preference for one or another technique. It is the consultant who decides what play materials to offer the child, and the art of these meetings lies in the consultant's capacity to adapt to the child's responses. However, over and above the question of *means* of communication, the most crucial factor in these consultations is the consultant's ability to convey to the child that he *wants* to learn of the child's experiences. Winnicott described this aptly and succinctly: "In the therapeutic consultation the material becomes specific and acutely interesting since the client soon begins to feel that understanding may perhaps be available and that communication at a deep level may become possible" (1971b, p. 7).

CHAPTER THREE

Child and parent interacting

In the cases described in this chapter, we can see one or both parents becoming actively involved in the interviews. Are they trying to maximize whatever help their child obtains from my input? Are they trying to protect the child from any possible influence from my words which might go against their opinions? Do they welcome this unfamiliar kind of intervention? Are they attending simply to pacify some impatient referrer? It is very important to have an open mind regarding these questions. The fact that the child has been brought to the interview signifies that the parents have responded to some motivation of their own to expose themselves and their child to this kind of scrutiny, the precise nature of which may be completely unknown to them. But the actual nature of their motivation has to be explored, since this will play a major role in planning what help to give the child.

There is no doubt that each of us is influenced by preconceived ideas, whether originating from our studies or from our personal lives. Meeting a child with his parents will, inevitably, arouse feelings in us that often take the form of opinions that an observer might consider judgemental and unwarranted. This is *par excellence* a situation where "gut feelings" or intuitions can be quite overwhelming and can endanger clarity of thinking. It is, therefore, most important not to dismiss a single one of these impressions, opinions, flash ideas, intuitions—or whatever other name we might want to give them—and, instead, proceed to put them to the test of further observation of the contributions of each member of the family. The image of the child as victim or of a parent as intrusive, self-centred, and deaf to the child's needs can occur much too often when seeing a family, but if we want to understand the family dynamics and elicit the nature of the roles that each one plays to keep it in place, then we must keep under repeated scrutiny each opinion we form of their contributions to the meeting.

In "Angela's" case, her mother was very keen to obtain help for her, but there was to be a limit to this intervention. While Mrs A welcomed the removal of Angela's symptoms, she had a very deep bond with the child and felt very threatened at the thought of this being in any way jeopardized. It can be quite a difficult situation for the consultant to believe that the child requires further professional input, whether investigative or therapeutic, and find that parents do not agree with such a recommendation. It is easy enough to put one's views on record, both voicing this to the parents and writing to the referrer, but there are times when difficult ethical issues may become involved, as when parents explicitly forbid any contact with another doctor. Angela's apparent communication difficulties were not easy to assess in our meetings, and I was left hoping that her teachers would take this up later if her subsequent development showed that this was necessary.

"Bob" proved an unexpected success. Late-adolescent bed-wetters are a difficult therapeutic challenge, but here I was helped by parents who could allow Bob to find his way to a cure, even if they did not fully grasp the unconscious reasons that had made them collude with and perhaps foster Bob's problem. From his point of view, he had an organic fault and his parents were showing their kindness and love by ensuring that he did not suffer unnecessary pain and humiliation—but both parents also had problems over their capacity for self-control, and this particular private interpretation of their son's difficulties (of which Bob was, obviously, not consciously aware) could only force them to sympathize with his lack of self-control. When Bob "accepted" that he had no organic damage, he could move to improvement, but what must be recognized is the fact that the parents were able to see his symptoms in a different light and, as a consequence, now gave him the stimulus and support he needed—not to maintain, but to overcome his symptom.

"Claude's" story depicts the ideal mother, who is able to take on board another person's view of her son, submit this to scrutiny, and gradually change her view of the situation, not out of blind belief in the doctor but through observing her son's efforts to overcome his difficulties. It should be noted how Mrs C chose to keep me out of further interviews; I would like to think that this was not out of any resentment or hostility but, rather, due to her wish to feel that her son could progress further without outside help.

"Daniel" makes a very amusing story. I will argue that the boy's problems followed from the conflicting injunctions he was receiving from his parents. The idea of "mixed messages" as a source of confusion has now become widely accepted, but I believe that many colleagues would argue that, whatever the parental input, this boy must have had some conflict over his instinctual impulses. This is a most interesting case in which we might argue over the unconscious motivation behind a particular behaviour; however, such investigation would require further interviews, which were not possible in this case. I happen to believe that children, as much as adults, can engage in repetitive behaviours (e.g., tics, obsessional rituals) that, even if there was a true reason that first originated them, come later to lose this meaning and become "meaningless" actions. Even if we leave out such a theory, the growing literature on infant psychiatry has been demonstrating how children's behaviour can change as soon as the parents understand the impact that their words and attitudes have on the child.

"Edward's" case shows us how deeply the child's progress depends on parental influences. Mrs E sought help for his bowel problems, but she believed that his enuresis was not a difficulty requiring professional help—and she was not prepared to change her mind over this. The interviews present fascinating examples of how a child will convey the content of his unconscious conflicts and how the mother's understanding of her son's anxieties signified that he could now overcome his problem. The subsequent reluctance to help Edward achieve bladder continence raises very difficult issues over establishing some prognosis for his later development, but this is a problem that consultants have to learn to live with.

"Jane's" interviews demonstrate the subtlety and complexity of a mother–daughter relationship. An intelligent, loving, and sensitive mother, Mrs J happens also to have an unconscious of her own, and our meetings showed her struggles to reconcile her intellectual understanding of Jane's needs with her own views on herself and her world. Jane did derive benefits from our meetings, but it would be difficult to predict how she would go through adolescence and negotiate the need to move from dependence to self-sufficiency.

Angela

Angela was first referred to the clinic when she was 25 months old. When she attended the health centre for a routine developmental check up, her mother, Mrs A, complained that Angela was presenting increasing difficulties with her eating. The community paediatrician wrote:

> "Angela has an eating problem. She survives on numerous snacks during the day and will only take a couple of mouthfuls of food at meal times. Mother says that she has used various approaches to try and get Angela to eat at meal times. This problem started at around 9 months of age and has not improved. Angela has managed, in spite of all this, to sustain good weight gain, remaining just above the 50th centile since the age of 9 months. My impression is that her mother is a sensible person and she does seem to have approached this problem in a reasonable manner."

An appointment was sent to Mrs A, but she failed to attend. We spoke to the referring doctor and to the family's health visitor, and we were told that it might be best not to pursue the referral at that point. One year later, Angela was referred again. The GP told us that Angela, now just over 3 years old, had had an eye test some months earlier, during which she was shown a picture of a fly, and since then had a severe "fly phobia" and was terrified of seeing them. She would cry and "pinch herself, refusing to go into any room until she is reassured that there are no flies there".

This time, Angela and Mrs A did attend. Angela curled up in mother's lap and refused to speak to me. It was Mrs A who recounted Angela's difficulties. The little girl was recovering from German measles, and I thought that this might be a factor in producing her clinging and her reluctance to answer any questions. Angela was an attractive child, modestly but neatly dressed, and I could see in her eyes that she was paying attention to every detail of our conversation. For her part, Mrs A was happy to hold Angela lovingly, while trying to answer my questions. After a while, I suggested to Angela that she might perhaps make a drawing; she closed her eyes, and Mrs A held her just that little bit more closely, giving the impression that there might be here an element of over-protection. Mrs A continued to answer my questions, and after a few more minutes Angela shifted her position and it was clear that she was ready to move away from her mother's lap; indeed, she went to the little desk where I kept paper and various kinds of pens.

Both Mrs A and I were quite near the desk, so that we could observe Angela's drawing. She made something of a circle, in which she inserted various features and announced that this was a picture of her father; it looked quite strange, but I made no comment. Angela then said she was going to draw her mother, but now Mrs A became an active participant, asking Angela for each detail of her face. Angela, obligingly, drew in the eyes, nose, and so on, and this did look more like a drawing of a face. As Angela developed this drawing, I was asking Mrs A to give me some information about herself and her husband. They had been married for about eight years, and Mrs A had had some difficulty with conceiving. Mrs A felt that considerable anxiety had surrounded Angela from birth, and this had caused her to be "a spoilt little girl". Mrs A added, laughing in a rather self-deprecatory way, that Angela's child-minder was very strict, "which must be good for Angela".

Mrs A told us that she worked part time in a supermarket and that her husband had an office job. Though both parents had several siblings, they were aware of the possibility that Angela might remain an only child. Mrs A told me that Angela had long been afraid of flies and spiders, but the incident at the optician's had added a more dramatic level to her anxieties. Angela had "screamed the place down [the optician's surgery]" when she saw a 3-D fly on one of the testing machines, and she now refused to enter any room from the moment she saw a fly there. One of the parents had to kill the fly, and Angela would then examine it—but a complication emerged at this point, with Mrs A telling me that she herself was also very frightened of flies and spiders. Angela was following the conversation, and I was puzzled by the difference between her alert, shining eyes and the general low-key, slow, immature movements of her body and her general demeanour. Her drawing also seemed very immature, in light of my impression of a child who could follow the adults' dialogue so attentively.

Angela now moved away from the paper and began to play with the dolls' house. She took off the roof with competent, dextrous movements and began to pick up pieces of furniture, which she proceeded to lift and drop into the opening left by the removal of the roof. This was definitely not the noise-provoking actions that some children will carry out—"attention-seeking behaviour", as it tends to be called. Angela picked up some piece of furniture, looked towards her mother and myself, smiled, and dropped it into the house. She clearly wanted to make sure that we were watching her actions. I asked Angela what she was trying to do, what was happening to the various pieces, who was throwing them—and several more questions that remained without answer.

I was puzzled by Angela's play, but Mrs A was even more puzzled by my determination to make something out of it. I just could not figure out what Angela was showing me/us, and I commented on my impression that there was something in Angela's eyes and in her facial expression when throwing the various bits of furniture that made me feel that she was not performing (with her drawings and now with the play with the wooden toys) at the level of her potential. To my surprise, Mrs A smiled and said that she had also noticed that "Angela seems to be acting more babyish than at home". This confirmation made me think that Angela might, quite unconsciously, be recreating some experience for which she lacked the vocabulary to articulate. I asked Angela if she might perhaps be showing us something that happens in her dreams: could it be that frightening things kept falling down in her dreams? Angela smiled coyly, nodded, and said a quiet "Yes". As soon as she said this, she sat down on a little chair and began to play with the furniture inside the house, now trying to organize it in some attractive way, like any other ordinary 3-year-old might do. She arranged the furniture and then brought several miniature "people" to sit around a table and enjoy a meal together, making it look like a family meal.

I did not really know how to relate all this to flies and spiders. I decided to call Mrs A's attention to the way in which Angela had repeatedly checked on her following each detail of her play, and, predictably, I was told that probably any child of that age would do the same. I gave what I thought was another example of the same kind of interaction, pointing to Angela's drawing of her mother's face: I wanted to avoid any impression of finding fault with Mrs A's behaviour, so I stressed how Angela cued her into dictating every detail of the face, much in contrast with the way in which she had drawn her father's face. Mrs A, rather reluctantly, agreed with my interpretation. When I thought that she had understood my point, I urged her to try to force Angela to follow her own inclination, whatever was involved, instead of giving her any form of guidance as to how to proceed. I added that there was a possibility that Angela might be following the same pattern over the issue of flies and spiders—that is, Angela might be indicating *fear* as a testing out of the mother's reaction to her feelings. If this was the case, then each time Mrs A reacted in a protective way, Angela was bound to believe that there was, indeed, something dangerous that she had to be defended from. Mrs A smiled politely, but I noticed that Angela had followed our conversation and, however much she could have understood of it, also had a warm, quiet smile on her face.

We had to stop, and we arranged a follow-up appointment; however, this was postponed by Mrs A, who claimed an unexpected family commitment. They came to see me again nearly two months later. The only reference to flies or spiders was Mrs A mentioning that it was no longer a problem. She said that immediately after our first meeting, Angela had become "a different child, her normal self". Both parents had noticed that she was "brighter and happier". Angela sat quietly, smiling occasionally but still refusing to engage with several attempts I made to talk to her. Eventually, Mrs A said that they had a new problem: Angela kept crying in her sleep, and all attempts to discover why this was happening had proved unsuccessful.

I suggested that Angela might perhaps like to make a drawing. I gave her some felt-tip pens and paper. She chose a yellow pen and looked up to her mother's face. I promptly signalled to Mrs A to refrain from telling Angela what to draw, and the mother smiled like a child caught red-handed just about to infringe some rule. Angela drew an irregular oval shape and moved back from the desk. She looked round, making sure that we were watching her. She leant forward towards the paper, still holding the pen, and this time she moved briskly away: the body movement pointed to fear or some similar emotion, even though her face showed a mischievous smile. She repeated these movements again, and by the third time round her body was contorted, as if in terror. I asked her what she had drawn, and this time she told me it was "a moo-cow". Before saying anything to Angela, I checked with Mrs A whether she had observed how Angela had made her drawing, particularly the body movements she had made. Very calmly, Mrs A confirmed that she had seen all this and added that she could explain what was going on.

Only a few days earlier, the family had gone on a drive to the country and at one point had suddenly come upon a herd of cows being moved along a road—and this had terrified Angela. As far as I could tell, Mrs A had not made any connection between Angela's behaviour (perhaps we can say "her body language") and the story she had told me. Apparently, from her point of view, she wanted me to know why a "moo-cow" had been drawn. I said that Angela had treated *the drawing* as if it was a real cow. Mrs A did not hide her disbelief—and anyway, even if I was right, how could this interpretation be relevant? I explained that with the drawing and her reaction, Angela might be showing us what was happening in her dreams. Angela nodded vigorously and said an emphatic "Yes". Very significantly, Mrs A now smiled in a way that, very eloquently, indicated that if Angela had confirmed my interpretation, then this sufficed for her to recognize and accept that this was correct. Angela must have read her mother's face in the same way as I did, because she moved away from the desk and went over to snuggle into her mother's lap.

Mrs A commented that "it was quite astonishing" that a little 3-year-old could find a way of conveying her experiences to me, even when lacking the words to express them. They left quite happily, and we learnt some weeks later from the health visitor that Angela had not had any further problems and that Mrs A kept telling people of the "magical" interchange between Angela and myself.

We heard from Angela and Mrs A again, two years later. Angela was again having nightmares, and Mrs A's anxiety was heightened by the fact that a crisis situation had developed at school. Somehow, Angela's teachers thought she was colour blind and also presented a speech defect; apparently, Mrs A had tried to argue with them that neither assertion appeared justified, but the teachers insisted on medical checks being carried out. Ophthalmic examination proved negative, but Angela still had to have the speech assessment. Probably because of the success of our earlier meetings, Mrs A requested a new appointment with me.

Angela seemed to recognize me, but she was just as monosyllabic as when we first met. Mrs A, for her part, remained enmeshed with Angela, quite incapable of keeping herself back whenever she gave the slightest indication of needing or wanting her mother's help. Angela had grown and seemed a confident child, but all my questions were answered with an "I don't know . . .", which might vary in tone, but not in words. But each time, she would look towards her mother, who promptly plunged into some kind of explanation. It was clear that Mrs A's anxiety was growing exponentially. I would guess that it was this brand of helplessness on Angela's part that had raised the teachers' concern, but it was quite possible that the teachers also saw her mother's level of anxiety as a further factor in Angela's difficulties.

As two years earlier, I resorted to pens and paper. Luckily, Angela accepted my suggestion. She drew a boat, lying tilted on its side. I tried many different questions to elicit what exactly that boat was meant to represent, but all I got was "I don't know". Eventually, she said it was "a blue and red boat"—I commented that she had used other colours, which she confirmed but could not (or would not) clarify why she had only chosen red and blue to name the boat. Very slowly and reluctantly, Angela recognized that she had forgotten to draw any water around the boat, but did not add it. Then she said it was on some path, though to me it looked as if the boat was floating on air, with no features around it to give any clue to its location. "When the wind blows it sails faster . . . when the wind is slow, it goes slow . . . when it rains, the people jump out of the boat on to the path." More questions from me—anything happening? Or had anything already happened? The boat was so tilted, why? Was it lost? Is it in the sea? Then, rather unexpectedly, Angela said the boat had fallen over because the wind had blown too fast—and added, "end of story". I was truly stuck. "You said people jumped on the path—what will they do?" "They work." So, not knowing what else to say, I asked, "What kind of story is this: is it funny or sad?", and she replied without hesitation, "It's sad, because of the boat . . .".

I asked whether she had seen this story in a book or on television? Had she made it up herself? Or could it be a dream? Having answered my questions in the negative, she now answered without delay: "It's a dream I had." Because Angela had said that it was the boat's situation that made for sadness, I ventured an interpretation asking her whether she was perhaps afraid of being left alone, like the boat. Angela smiled, coyly, but her mother promptly jumped, telling me that only a few days ago Angela had told her of a dream: they had seen some balloons in the street when returning home from school, and in her dream Angela *was holding on to a balloon by its string, while the balloon appeared to take her away into the air*. I put the two explanations together and suggested that Angela might be afraid of not being held, or being allowed to get out of reach, of losing contact. Poor Mrs A was now beyond herself—could this fear be related to her now working full-time? Angela goes to a childminder after school, "but I'm never late!" and, soon, "Do you think I should stop working? Would she be less afraid?"

I explained that it was unlikely that we were dealing with actual events that called for immediate remediation; I suggested that Angela knew quite well that her mother would not neglect her, but it could have happened that one day Mrs A was a bit late and Angela had formed the impression that she might not come any more. Angela, who had not missed a single word of this conversation, now nodded vigorously. Mrs A now remembered that the childminder's son had "only the other day" joked with Angela that her mother would not come for her. Curiously, exactly as two years earlier, Angela now relaxed quite visibly and moved over to the other side of the table to play with various toys.

I discussed with Mrs A what to do next. I could not think that any tests would reveal any particular physical abnormality, but I encouraged her to comply with the teachers' requests. I explored the possibility of offering Angela some psychotherapy, but Mrs A was quite determined not to have any more interventions than those she decided were absolutely indispensable. She refused a follow-up appointment with the powerful argument that, as she had already come back for further help when she thought this necessary, she could reassure me that she would do so again, if the need arose.

Comments

I feared that Angela would have to struggle very hard to achieve some independence from her mother. Mrs A had a very low level of tolerance for anxiety, particularly where Angela was involved, and this made it virtually impossible for her to appreciate Angela's behaviour as pertaining to a separate person. I thought it would be inappropriate to enquire why Mrs A had decided to work full-time—any question might lead her to imagine I disapproved of her doing this. Anyway, "working full-time" was probably just one example of circumstances that made Mrs A feel extremely guilty when Angela showed signs of distress, and, as our interviews showed, her own emotional turmoil only led to further anxiety in Angela. Fortunately, the two series of interviews were able to break the vicious circle in the present crises: Angela could understand what her dreams meant, and finding her fears put into words seemed to relieve her symptoms, whilst Mrs A seemed to find my words reassuring enough for her to continue what was, undoubtedly, her good-enough care of Angela. However, I would anticipate further crises as Angela made her progress through late childhood and adolescence.

Bob

Sixteen-year-old Bob came to see me with his parents, Mr and Mrs B. His family doctor asked me to see Bob because he was still enuretic, and this made for great difficulties in his school and general social life. The interview lasted two hours, and it would be impossible to convey in detail how each participant contributed to the discussion: this was very lively and easy-going, moving from the formal to the "jokey", with many unexpected discoveries which gave rise to amusement just as often as to shock and pain. Bob was a well-built adolescent with no particular distinguishing features. He was reasonably intelligent, not very articulate, and quite shy, perhaps only too aware of the circumstances in which he was seeing me. His parents were a normal working-class couple, laughing and talking with the respect they would show a doctor and yet with the warmth and ease they might experience when meeting neighbours or friends.

I first tried to get Bob to tell us how he saw his problems. In a voice loaded with embarrassment, he said that he was still wetting his bed. He had tried many techniques and had recently had some slight improvement after taking Imipramine, but the wetting still continued. He explained how this affected his social life—for example, he never accepted invitations to stay at friends for the night or went on school outings. To the best of his knowledge, there had never been a time when he was dry at night. I presume he considered my response sympathetic enough, because he seemed to gain courage to add that he had an additional problem, in that every so often during the day he felt an urge to urinate that was so pressing that he had to leave the classroom or interrupt any activity to avoid wetting himself.

Mr and Mrs B indicated that they were quite aware of this problem. First, they simply acknowledged its existence, but gradually they embarked on accounts of the way in which this urinary frequency affected the family life. From some nearly factual stories about mealtimes being interrupted, they eventually moved to descriptions of car and/or train journeys—and by then the psychiatric social worker and I were laughing as much as all of them were. Car journeys would be interrupted "every 2 miles" and the family would wait until Bob found a suitable place to urinate; they sometimes missed train connections while waiting for Bob to discover where a toilet was available. The wider family had long made jokes out of the invariable lateness that characterized the Bs' visits. We were told in great detail and with considerable laughter how parents and siblings would stay at the door, waiting for Bob to feel satisfied that he had emptied his bladder, before he managed to leave home.

It was quite difficult to find the language to shift from this comedy atmosphere to its painful implications. I asked the parents how they had come to accept the incredible manoeuvres they performed in order to fit in with Bob's needs. I was promptly put in my place: how could a parent behave any differently *vis-à-vis* a needy child? And they gave me other examples of how they dealt with their children's lives—they obviously did not distinguish between a wish and a need, and they painted a picture where the children were left to find their own way in life, as if any imposition or demand on the parents' part would represent an intrusion to be avoided. Firmness or discipline seemed taboo, and to an outsider Mr and Mrs B seemed to have fostered a climate that could not but lead to a chaotic style of life. Nevertheless, when we talked about Bob's younger siblings, it seemed that they had flourished in this same atmosphere. They were described as efficient, neat, task-oriented, and invariably successful at school and in other areas of their lives. For some reason, the manner in which Mr and Mrs B treated their children had not affected Bob's siblings in the same manner in which it had affected him.

I tried to explore with Bob how he experienced his problems. It turned out that he was totally convinced that there was some anatomical fault in his urinary apparatus. Considering his age and the fact that he had studied some biology at school, I asked him to describe his image of what micturition involved. Not surprisingly, he did not know about bladder sphincters, let alone about voluntary and involuntary functions. We focused on kidneys, bladder, and penis. Bob knew that, however frequent his urge to urinate, he had never actually wet himself during the day. Gradually he perceived that this fact indicated that there could not be any organic deficit underlying his symptoms. He was not just relieved, he was quite enthusiastic.

Mr and Mrs B followed our conversation with some interest, though they looked quite puzzled, as if not quite seeing how it could be relevant. But I thought they were shifting their positions on their chairs, as if finding it difficult to understand why they had to be kept in the room. Indeed, Mr B eventually could not contain himself any longer, and, with the tone of voice one associates with a little schoolboy addressing the class-teacher, he asked me for permission to leave the room to smoke a cigarette, since he had "not had a cigarette for some three hours now." Well, this was an unexpected demonstration of the fact that Bob was not the only one to struggle with urges and self-control! At this point, it became very difficult to ignore how overweight Mrs B was and not consider that she also struggled with the same difficulty to impose control over physical urges. I did manage to comment on the similarity between Mr B's request and Bob's demands that the family should stop the car along the motorway, but I thought it would not be wise (or prudent?) to remark on Mrs B's weight.

But Mr B's decision to smoke his cigarette led us to discuss the fundamental issue of what is and what is not acceptable. This interview took place many years before smoking became such a condemnable habit as it is nowadays, but the very fact that Mr B had asked me for permission underlined the point that one person's need may impinge on another one's views. This was the much-needed cue to look into the parents' attitudes towards Bob's urinary problems. Now, however, Mr and Mrs B showed a different facet of their personalities: they felt accused and became quite angry that they might be found at fault. I tried to show that there was no question of allocating blame, but Bob took over. This was now suddenly a self-confident youngster, as if he had at last found it possible to let us know that he had thoughts and opinions of his own.

Bob argued that what his parents thought was kindness and tolerance towards his wetting and its frequency had, in fact, led to his being confused about it. "If a child goes about the house scribbling on the walls, you would expect the parents to teach the child that that kind of behaviour is not acceptable!" I thought that Mrs B understood Bob's argument, but Mr B was quite dumbfounded by this, as if the meaning of Bob's words had escaped him and only the notion of "an outburst"—that is, another episode of incontinence—counted to him.

Bob looked pleased. Perhaps he found it gratifying that the psychiatric social worker and I seemed to have "taken his side", even if his parents appeared not to have understood his grievances. But Mr and Mrs B felt they needed something more tangible to take away with them. They asked for a prescription: what should they do? How should they respond to Bob? I was only a new doctor, coming on the scene after a long list of physicians and specialists who had conducted innumerable tests and examinations—only talking? What could this achieve?

I was quite determined to keep away from the model of "illness", believing that to behave now "like a doctor does" would only lead Bob to fall back on the notion of there being "something wrong with his body". Furthermore, I did not really think that these parents, however devoted and loving they undoubtedly were, would be able to change their approach to Bob. I thought that I had to concentrate on helping Bob to build up his self-confidence, and I asked the parents to forgive me if I did not give them any definite recommendation. I suggested that they should just think over all the things we had discussed, and I asked Bob to come to see me again. However, I asked him to make a diary, noting which nights he had a wet bed.

Bob came to see me three weeks later. Mrs B also came along. Bob had counted twenty nights without "accidents", and both he and his mother were very happy with this. Mrs B was particularly proud, and she stressed how much Bob had gained in confidence as the days had gone by. He was more outgoing, his tone of voice showed more firmness, he was seeing much more of his peers, and altogether he seemed a happier fellow. Bob beamed at all this praise.

Bob came to see me once more, a month later. This time, he could barely disguise his reluctance at being there. He now counted thirty-six consecutive nights without any wetting, and, since the one accident, he had had a further twenty-four dry nights. These figures were put forward as if they were jewels or trophies; they obviously meant an enormous amount to him. He now expected the final verdict to come from me, and I had no doubt that the best prize would be for me to confirm that he could now proceed on his own. We parted with a warm handshake, and Bob knew he could see me again if, and only if, this was necessary—that is, if he ever wished to do so.

It was only from the GP that I learnt some months later that Bob had not had any further urinary problems.

Comments

Contrary to my other cases, here I did not gain any knowledge of Bob's unconscious fantasies about his symptoms; I suppose his idea of having some physical damage was the cue to some pathogenic fantasy, but it seems that the clarification that this fault was non-existent sufficed to remove his anxiety. But, no doubt, this case illustrates the power of family dynamics to produce symptoms that dramatically affect one individual member of that family. Assuming that the B family had problems over impulse control, we might postulate that Mrs B's weight and Mr B's smoking represented manifestations of this conflict. However, it seemed that they did not consider these features as pathological, but when Bob built his own complex of symptoms around his urination, this became the focus of the family concerns. The consultations seem to have freed him from the family conflict, but I have no information on how this affected the dynamics of the whole family.

Claude

Claude, aged 3 years, was referred to a consultant paediatrician during a visit to his grandparents, and this doctor wrote his report to the family's usual GP:

"Claude seems to have been a lively and happy boy until the parents returned from a three-week holiday three months ago. A few days after coming home, his mother tried to get Claude to come out of nappies and use the potty, but despite running around with the bare bottom he would not use the toilet and withheld urine until he had pants on later, at which point he wet himself. After a few days of this behaviour, Claude became emotionally distraught, listless, anorectic and just wanting to go to bed. He was also clingy and difficult when he started screaming at night. There had been no obvious reason why Claude would not use the toilet or potty: no frights or negative enforcement and he had seen his parents and older sister using the toilet. He would not even micturate outside in the garden, wanting to hide in the corner with pants on before he would do it. Since this time, Claude's behaviour has really changed quite a lot. He is now emotionally labile with tantrums. He easily becomes distressed and will not go to other people. A neighbour tried to help with the potty-training and Claude is said to become completely hysterical. His mother has been particularly concerned about it because of the lassitude and poor appetite with weight loss."

After a thorough physical examination that excluded any pathology, the doctor recommended that "we should forget about potty-training for the moment" and suggested that the GP might want to refer Claude to a "clinical psychologist, mostly so that Mother has reassurance about the way she manages Claude and to plan for re-establishing potty-training".

The paediatrician had obviously taken great care to assess the situation, and his views are quite typical of similar consultations. Physically, nothing can be found; the child is considered to be reacting to some traumatic experience and has now developed a behaviour problem, and therefore the mother must be helped to cope with her unnecessary worries, which should enable her to put the child back on the normal development track. This doctor gave good advice, since "forgetting about potty training for the moment" would reduce the vicious circle of unhappiness, failure, and pain that child and mother had become caught up with. However, the rationale of "referring to a clinical psychologist" reflects the belief that only "wrong" or "faulty" behaviour is at stake and that this would be corrected through some form of retraining.

The family's GP wrote that "a very distraught parent came to see me as since she attempted to potty train her child some six weeks ago, which was a total disaster, the child's behaviour has become impossible and he is rejecting all normal convention, despite the parents showing no concern regarding the failure of the training programme". I wondered whether "parents showing no concern" was really congruous with "a very distraught parent came to see me", but then parents do seem to believe that children do not perceive any more than they are supposed to perceive.

The mother, Mrs C, brought Claude to see us. She was an attractive woman, clearly self-confident and treating her son warmly and sensitively. Claude was quite a small boy, very shy; he was absolutely fascinated by a young, blonde psychologist who worked with me and could not take his eyes away from her. I asked Mrs C how she had told Claude about our meeting, and she could not see the relevance of the question, simply telling me that she had said they were coming to see "the doctor". The psychologist asked Claude some questions, and he mumbled monosyllables in reply.

I had put pens and paper on a table, together with a dolls' house and some toys, and Claude quickly moved towards the pens. Mrs C happily began to tell us the story described in the consultant's letter, but one could sense the intensity of the feelings of distress that both Claude and his mother had experienced. While his mother was talking to us, Claude began to play with the pens, naming each colour, and then he made some lines that looked more like smudges on one of the sheets of paper (Figure 3.1). Claude pointed to some lines in the middle of these shapes and said this was the first letter of his sister's name.

Claude now took another sheet of paper and drew a long green line, named it "green", and proceeded to do a similar line named "red"; for some reason, he was now giggling, and he drew a further

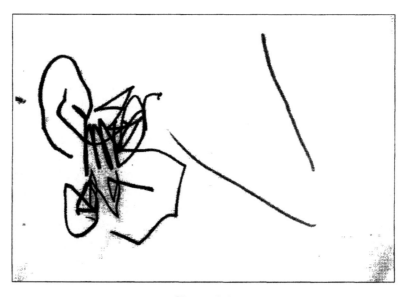

Figure 3.1

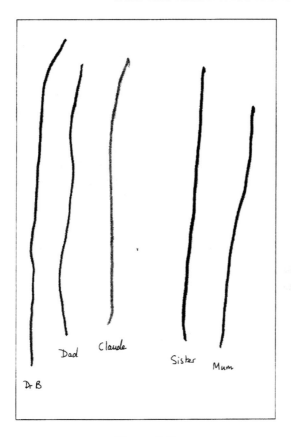

Figure 3.2

"black" line (Figure 3.2). The mother asked him what these lines represented, and he first said they were "lamp-posts" and Mrs C recognized that he was having fun, teasing us with some game that was not being revealed. But then Claude declared that the "green" line was himself and the "red line" was his sister. We could not but join in the laughter and Claude now added that "black" was his mother. Mrs C must have decided to defuse the growing excitement that Claude was showing and moved back to her account of recent events. I had also asked her to tell us some information about herself and the family, and she was giving me this information as well. But Claude continued with his game, and, having drawn a "brown" line, he insistently tried to get his mother's attention and then informed her that this was his father. I thought I should help myself here and asked permission to put initials on each line, to remind myself of whom they represented. Claude was quite happy I should do this, and, when I finished, he promptly did a further "brown" line and said this was me. Mrs C told him my name and he found it quite hilarious, repeating it with ample laughter.

I thought I recognized the theme of Claude's lines, since he had so clearly separated the males from the females, whilst making them all look exactly the same as each other. But *my* problem now was to discover some way of helping Claude to clarify what was behind those straight, vertical lines.

But perhaps I should recount some of the history of the family that I had gathered from Mrs C while Claude was making his drawing. She described her husband and herself as journalists. She added that he travels all the time, which led me to comment that "he must be a successful journalist!"—"well", she answered, "a journalist who works a lot . . ."—and we both laughed, she amused and I rather apologetic for my *faux pas*. I was told that Mr C was older than his wife. Mrs C stopped work when her daughter was born; she was now just over 5 years old and attended a local primary school, where she was doing very well. Claude was also due to start at that school's nursery, and the teachers had accepted quite well the fact that he was still in nappies. We discussed family routines, and I learnt that the family had an easy-going attitude over baths and toilets, so that the children had always been free to go there when either parent was having a bath or using the toilet. However, Claude was noticeably more interested than his sister was in watching his parents during those activities, though when it came to his urinating, whatever stratagems the parents used to persuade him to use the toilet, he managed to hold his urine until he had the nappy put on him. Mrs C gave me many examples of these episodes, where all participants had gone through endless arguments, promises, tears, but eventually found that they had to capitulate to Claude's pleas.

As far as I could see, Mrs C had adjusted very well to her husband's style of life. She was a warm, caring mother, and it was obvious that she was keen to help Claude, but she could only put into practice those techniques that friends, health visitors, doctors had recommended—all of which bypassed whatever anxiety the boy was harbouring.

Trying to devise some way of getting Claude to comment on "boys" and "girls", I voiced my wish that he would draw these figures, but he clearly would be unable to achieve this, so I asked Mrs C if she could, perhaps, help me out. She smiled and said that this was no problem. Claude himself offered her some felt-tip pens, choosing a colour for each picture that he proceeded to "request" his mother to draw. Claude was dictating details and when, at one point, Mrs C commented that something was missing, I asked her not to do this but, instead, only follow the boy's instructions. She indicated that this made sense.

Claude started with a boy, himself, in blue (Figure 3.3). First, he asked for "legs", and Mrs C wanted to know whether these should be fat or thin. "Fat", he answered. Then followed the ears, mouth, eyes, nappy/pants (he called them "pants"); he also asked for "a napkin", which he explained was to be used for breakfast time. Mrs C was intrigued that he was not asking for arms or tummy or the shape of the head, but by then Claude had already given her the grey pen, asking her to draw "Mummy".

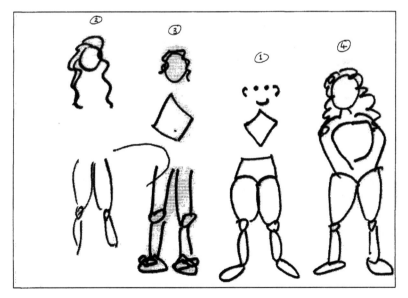

Figure 3.3

"Mummy" was even more incomplete than the first "boy", but fortunately Mrs C did not comment or make suggestions. Then came "daddy", drawn in red, again with no arms and with the angular-shaped napkin. I cannot remember whether I or Mrs C asked Claude how he would draw "a girl": no arms again, but the same long hair as "mummy", though this picture had a body and a circular napkin.

I asked Mrs C for comments on the drawings. She said that she was puzzled by the missing parts of the various bodies, but she herself added that probably Claude might not be able to explain the rationale for his unusual way of depicting the various members of the family. Claude was quietly following this conversation; he seemed pleased with his mother's drawing, but he was not volunteering any comments. I asked the psychologist for comments, and, after a pause, she said that "one gets the impression that he has some conflict about the genital area . . ." Mrs C was surprised, but as she concentrated, trying to figure out the plausibility of this idea, there was an expression of amusement in her eyes, as if she could see the logic of my colleague's opinion. And at this point, I took the plunge into the kind of interpretation that must read extraordinarily forceful, if not intrusive. I can only state, in mitigation, that this was one of those cases where one can feel most intensely that child and parent are totally aware of what is on show, even if unable to find the words to articulate their understanding. Of course, when addressing a family, I use language that the child can comprehend, but this is rather difficult to reproduce after the event, probably because, even as I put forward my ideas, I am constantly checking that the child is following my words and indicating some kind of understanding.

I said that the original straight lines (Figure 3.2) showed that Claude *can* separate the sexes, but his fuller pictures (Figure 3.3) depicted them all as having no genitals; in fact, only the drawing of Claude had pants/nappy covering his genital area. Using the word familiar to Claude (supplied by Mrs C), I said that he seemed to be afraid that he would lose "his pee-pee", since he imagined that his sister and his mother had lost theirs—hence, the nappy for protection. Claude had a vague grin on his face, but Mrs C was very thoughtful, finally saying: "I did wonder that he seemed to be more involved with us than with his father . . ."

I asked Claude how his father urinated and he replied "standing up", so I suggested that maybe he would find it possible to "pee" in that standing position. Mrs C promptly said that she had tried that, many times, without success. But I now noticed that Claude was definitely holding his hand against his penis, and I suggested to Mrs C she might want to ask him what he thought of all that I had been saying. She did ask him, and, to the surprise of all of us, he said that his "pee-pee has already been taken away". I asked him if this was in fact so, but, rather embarrassed, he replied that it was there. I could only surmise that he believed he had already lost at least part of his penis, being then afraid that he might lose what was left of it.

We had ran out of time, and I explained to Mrs C that Claude's anxiety was not that uncommon. I added that, seeing that his present crisis had been linked to his parents' absence on holiday, it was also possible that Claude might be dreading his starting at nursery school. Therefore, it might be useful if Mrs C would perhaps continue her attempts to get him to use the toilet and help him to understand that going to nursery school and "peeing like his daddy" were both normal, positive steps in his growing up.

We had a second meeting one week later, when I was told that there was less anxiety and distress at home, but no change had occurred in Claude's behaviour. We discussed the various points that had emerged in our first meeting and we arranged to meet again in two weeks' time. However, the meeting was cancelled and a new appointment was agreed upon. This one was also cancelled, but this time I received a letter from Mrs C, in which she wrote:

"The toilet training has been a complete success. In the four weeks since our second meeting we had four accidents, all but one in bed and all but one in the first week. Since the beginning of the second week, we have been fine, including nights. We had a little trouble moving on to standing up to pee, but that is also sorted out now too, as has his unwillingness to use toilets away from home. The last step will be to stop using the clip-on toilet seat, but I see no rush, especially if that undermines his urge to be independent about his trips to the loo. I wanted to report our progress—there is obviously no need to have another appointment—and to thank you for your help. I am delighted the problem is behind us and that we got some insight into his difficulties, rather than just imposing socially acceptable behaviour over his worries."

Comments

Understandably, this letter has remained one of my most valued trophies and conclusive proof of the validity of my approach to these cases. Sadly, however, not all mothers are able to step back and reappraise what, in fact, determines their child's behaviour. Claude's "castration anxiety", to use the textbook diagnosis, is quite common among young boys, and many of these are taken on for long-term psychotherapy. In fact, enuresis itself is the target of an enormous variety of therapeutic approaches. Most, if not all, of these techniques can claim success after some kind of interval. From a statistical point of view, it is possible to argue that the majority of children will, at some point, achieve bladder control. A strictly pragmatic view of the situation seems to be that which treatment is prescribed for enuresis depends entirely on the professional who comes to be consulted. Urologists and surgeons will argue that each child should be "properly investigated" in case there is some underlying physical pathology, while some psychodynamically oriented practitioners will stress the need for "proper emotional support" for the child. In between these extremes, there is no end of medicines, machines, technical stratagems, and kindly advice that parents have to put into practice and the child has to endure.

I am always aware of the fact that, by the time most children come to see me, they have already been seen by the GP and, sometimes, by a paediatrician as well. I can therefore allow myself the luxury of knowing that a colleague has excluded any physical pathology; I confess that this does not lead me to blind belief in their diagnosis, but it certainly helps me to concentrate on emotional factors affecting child and parents.

Claude's case shows a very typical presentation where the child's symptom is seen as abnormal behaviour requiring correction, but, as a consequence, the parents' "corrective" behaviour is interpreted by the child as confirmation of his anxiety that some part of his body is being threatened. At this point, distress escalates and very complex feelings invade all participants—most of them simply aggravating and reinforcing the vicious circle between child and parents.

Understanding the nature of his anxiety seems to have helped Claude, but it is clear that his mother's totally different approach to him must have, at least initially, signified that his sense of being under some threat no longer seemed justified. Once this vicious circle is broken, the way is open for child and parents to resume their normal functioning.

Daniel

Daniel was 13 months old when, out of desperation, his parents agreed to see a child psychiatrist. Daniel was biting "everyone around him". They had tried to find some logic behind the biting, but without success. Daniel's choice of people to bite appeared to show no discernible preference; if most occasions followed "signs of anger or frustration", there were other times when there was no recognizable emotional affect before Daniel bit someone.

Daniel's parents were young professionals. Daniel's pregnancy and labour had been normal, and he was developing normally. He walked reasonably well, he understood very well words addressed to him, his articulation seemed clear, and his vocabulary was increasing in an age-appropriate manner. In my room, Daniel played with various toys, demonstrating good coordination and an appreciation of the function of each toy, which he handled very gently. At one point he asked his father to pick him up; he seemed to be paying attention to the flow of our conversation, but he did not appear controlling or demanding. Instead, with his desire satisfied, he now nestled his head quietly and lovingly into his father's shoulder, as if respecting the fact that his father was conversing with a stranger.

His parents, Mr and Mrs D, told me of the multitude of colleagues, friends, relations, health visitor, and doctor who had given them advice on how to help Daniel. Among other things, they had told him off, hit him, bitten him back, put strong-flavoured substances on his lips, put him in his cot, strapped him on his chair, and so forth—all to no avail. I was quite convinced, to judge from their account, that they did not really believe that I would ever manage to divine any new, miraculous technique that would be of use.

Considering Daniel's behaviour towards the toys, his parents, and myself, I was certain that this was an eminently educable, responsive child: his parents had clearly enabled him to deal with himself and the world with respect and consideration—with the glaring exception of the biting. My conclusion was that Daniel's biting had met some blind spot in his parents' view of the world or, to put it more correctly, in their view of how Daniel should relate to people around him. It followed that I should explore each parent's background and their attitudes about the biting.

Mrs D was a young Jewish woman who had moved to London after her marriage. She had been an active participant in the social movements of the 1960s. Overtly, she rejected ordinary conventions, and she had married Mr D against her parents' wishes: though not religious, he came from a Catholic family. However, some hesitations in her answers and the occasional change in the tone of her voice made me think that these could be indications that, for her, the transgression of customs and conventions might lead to conflict and perhaps even guilt. Mr D was the same age as his wife. He came to London for his university studies and made a successful career here. He also believed that a new society was needed, that previous generations must have failed as the Cold War and Vietnam had followed the Second World War. His childhood and adolescence had taught him that "survival and wellbeing were [each one's] responsibility". He was very conscious of the sense of loyalty to family and friends, but, like his wife, he argued for each individual's right to fight for himself.

Carefully, but with determination, I asked each parent to comment on Daniel's biting. Specifically, following my previous findings, I wanted them to concentrate on the problem of a child's duties to his elders and his rights to establish his own identity. It must be noted that I was taking advantage of the fact that these were parents who had given these issues considerable thought, even if not explicitly in terms of the upbringing of their beloved firstborn.

Mrs D felt that a child was entitled to try to gain possession of things he desired, but she also believed that a child had to learn to moderate his desires and accept that others also had wishes and rights. To some extent, Mr D could agree with this formulation, but he firmly believed that a child must not be allowed to learn that surrender and compliance are the rule of the world. They could both understand the concept of compromise, but as they focused on a growing child—their son—Mrs D felt that biting was a personal attack that transgressed the other person's integrity, whilst her husband believed that if his son had no other weapon at his disposal, then biting was a legitimate means of defence and self-assertion.

I translated all this for Mr and Mrs D: they were criticizing, reprimanding, punishing, disciplining Daniel, probably even using similar or the same words. However, each of them had very conflicting views about their son's behaviour. Mrs D was trying to bring up a child who was not bound to the Jewish values she professed to have left behind, but her injunctions that he stop biting others were essentially based precisely on those values. For his part, Mr D insisted Daniel stopped biting, but he deeply believed that, were Daniel to obey him, he might develop into the kind of human being whom Mr D despised—someone incapable of asserting his rights and fighting for his wishes.

Not surprisingly, Mr and Mrs D, in virtual unison, told me that I was talking nonsense: I was reading too much into what they had said; I was drawing inferences that they could admit were plausible but were of no relevance to the issue of their son's behaviour. They were trying hard to retain their politeness. I told them that I could not offer any proof of the validity of my interpretation, but I insisted that the only thing they could do to help Daniel was to discuss their views, as they had emerged in our meeting. I enumerated a long list of Daniel's behaviours during the meeting that were evidence of the many ways in which they had taught him to develop as a well-functioning child. All of this suggested that Daniel must be picking up from their words and behaviour about the biting that the *overt* message contained an underlying *covert* one that contradicted it, and this left him feeling confused about their *real, actual* expectations of him.

Mr and Mrs D refused my suggestion of a further appointment. They offered me the polite compromise of a telephone call to report on progress. A few days later, I received a call from Mrs D: she was amused, apologetic, and immensely puzzled—since the moment they left my room, David had not bitten anyone again. She did not know how this could possibly have happened, she said.

Comment

Contrary to the other cases in this book, I cannot say much about Daniel's unconscious ideas regarding his position in the world. We only have the evidence of his behaviour during my consultation and of the account his parents gave of his behaviour in daily life. This is behaviour that, from a psychoanalytic perspective, we would consider evidence of exaggerated hostile impulses, manifesting themselves through oral mechanisms; it is quite possible that the expression "oral sadistic" might be brought up, since Daniel was using his teeth as weapons against those around him, even if he could perceive the feedback that these others were being hurt by his bites.

It would be impossible to establish what was on Daniel's mind when he bit someone for the first time, but, as happens with many other children, an incidental piece of behaviour is somehow transformed into a habit—and by the time these children come to see us, we are supposed to make sense of a piece of behaviour that is not acceptable to parents or to the world at large. But how are we to interpret such behaviour? Is it proof of faulty development of sociability? Could it indicate a lack of awareness of the distinction between different objects? Is this early evidence of later pathology? As argued in other parts of this book, this diagnostic evaluation will depend entirely on the conceptual framework of the professional seeing the child. I took the line that Daniel was *responding* to a confusing injunction from his parents—this evaluation relies on seeing Daniel and his parents as part of a mutually influencing system of interactions, where a change in this interaction can bring about further changes in the other participants of the interrelating system.

According to the referrer, he was not consulted for further problems over Daniel. Unfortunately, I cannot report later follow-up contact with the D family, but it seems that the crisis that brought them to the consultation was overcome successfully.

Edward

The paediatrician asked me to see Edward when he was 3 years old because the boy's constipation had not responded to various drug treatments and the consultant found himself now facing the fact that complications that he could not have anticipated had developed. When he first saw Edward, the paediatrician established a programme of laxatives and diet, besides giving Edward's mother, Mrs E, detailed instructions as to how to help her son achieve a regular rhythm of emptying his bowels. At the second follow-up appointment, the mother's report produced intense alarm in the paediatrician. At one level of dosage, the drugs were producing "a powerful evacuation" with such mess that the mother felt that this was unfair on the child. At a smaller dosage, however, Edward was again holding back his stools, so that Mrs E had now "arranged the situation so that every third day she put Edward in the bath and encouraged him to empty his bowels into it". The paediatrician thought that this was not a simple case for a change of medicines, but still tried to convince Mrs E that making Edward defecate in the bath was unhygienic and educationally not desirable. Mrs E said she might agree with the hygiene aspect, but not otherwise. I do not really know how the discussion went, but eventually the paediatrician managed to persuade Mrs E that she should consult a child psychiatrist. Reluctantly, Mrs E agreed to see me.

Edward had achieved his developmental milestones quite normally, and by the age of 1½ years he was dry and clean. Some time after that, Edward began to show a reluctance to empty his bowels, and Mrs E turned to health visitors and doctors in search of effective advice. Various drugs and diets were tried; Edward was kept in nappies and encouraged to empty his bowels into them; progress charts with various rewards were attempted, but the problem persisted. In due course, Edward was referred to the consultant paediatrician.

At our first meeting, I was told a very painful family history. Mr E was in his 40s and had children from a previous marriage. His work involved travelling abroad, and his contact with Edward was rather limited. Mrs E was in her mid-30s. She had been married to a man who was keen to have children, but they had not managed to have any. At one point, after she had a brief affair, the couple decided to separate, but Mrs E soon discovered that she was pregnant. She was thrown into great emotional turmoil, since she barely knew the man whose child she was now carrying. In a painful meeting with her first husband, he pleaded with her to continue to live with him, as they would now have the child they so much wanted. But, after much thought, she decided that the child should live with his real father, and she left her husband. Sadly, however, having married Mr E, the new couple had never managed to build a stable relationship, and there were increasing difficulties in the marriage.

As I tend to do in all cases of bowel dysfunction, I enquired about the parents' bowel habits. It turned out that neither Mr nor Mrs E "paid much attention" to this; both just assumed that their bowels opened every second or third day. As for Edward, Mrs E told me how he would curl up on his belly in a "frog position", tightening up his legs; she believed that this was his way of ensuring that the faeces would not come out. Occasionally he would sit on the potty and defecate normally.

Edward had quickly made himself at home in my room. He explored several toys, and he smiled to me in a friendly manner, not giving many answers to my questions, but clearly making sure I was paying attention to his activities. He picked up some felt-tips and made some clumsy scribbles, but soon he was banging the crayons and making a loud noise that—he instructed me—I was supposed to jump at. Each time I jumped, he laughed, pleased and excited, only to repeat the game again. After a while, he stopped and moved away to the dolls' house: he was now quite silent, perhaps following the conversation I was having with his mother.

Mrs E had never had any experience with children before her son was born. She was a caring and loving mother, but she had no concept of a child's developing cognitive abilities. His words were taken at face value—that is, literally—and Mrs E just did not believe that Edward's play might have any meaning or that he might have feelings and thoughts that, at his age, he lacked the capacity to articulate. When I tried to suggest that Edward's sphincter difficulties might be linked to his feelings and ideas rather than to some physical factor which required diet and/or medication, she reacted with polite scepticism. After so many attempts at medical intervention which had invariably failed, she was willing to consider new interpretations, but she could not accept the idea that children might have feelings that could significantly influence the workings of their bodies.

I searched for some example that might convince Mrs E. I remembered Edward's game, demanding that I should jump when he made his noisy "bangs"; I suggested to his mother that those were the noises he feared his stools would make. Edward promptly pronounced a very clear "Yes!", but Mrs E argued, kindly but firmly, that he could not possibly have heard any noises, since "there was no bang" when he used the potty, the water, or the nappy. I laughed and admitted that she must be right, but it was still possible that Edward might have heard someone else or even heard an unrelated noise—or, who knows?—simply imagined a connection between faeces and noise: the fact remained that he had confirmed my suggestion. Mrs E could admit this, but she was not convinced.

We had run out of time, and I discussed with Mrs E the importance of sitting Edward on the toilet and trying to achieve a situation where he might develop a habit of defecating which would not be connected to fears or ideas of any kind. She asked me about drugs, and I said that this was something she must discuss with the paediatrician. Mrs E was puzzled by the whole interview but said she "would try".

I saw Edward and his mother again two weeks later. Both of them looked more relaxed, but there had not been any significant progress over Edward's problem. Mrs E and I sat on the same chairs we had occupied the previous time, and Edward explored the toys in the room. He took up some trains and the rails on which they could move; he built a circuit, putting a tunnel at one point, and began to make the trains move. He then built a smaller circle, retaining the tunnel, and now moved the little carriages, getting them to crash, making loud noises with his mouth. Time and again, a carriage would get stuck inside the tunnel, and this made Edward pick up a ruler nearby and then make "strenuous" and loud efforts to push the train out of the tunnel. Mrs E said Edward "enjoys the noise". Again, Mrs E was focusing on the overt behaviour and emphasizing the mechanical aspect of Edward's play. I was keen to help Edward convey to his mother what was troubling him, and to achieve this I had to put into words what I believed was the communication Edward was depicting through his play with the trains. Being careful to use a gentle tone of voice, I suggested to Mrs E that the circle and the tunnel might be a representation of Edward's idea of an anus. Mrs E was taken aback, but promptly and quietly asked Edward, "Is that your bottom?", to which he said, "*Yes*". In view of his confirmation, I pointed out how he kept getting a train stuck inside the tunnel and to his exaggerated efforts to push it out. I stressed the "stuck inside" and the "forcing out", adding that he was illustrating his anxiety about what happened inside himself and his fear of what would come out of him. Here, we had a significant change. To my surprise, Mrs E told me of a children's story that Edward keeps asking her to read to him: the story of Henry the Engine, a locomotive that gets stuck in a tunnel. Each time she gets to this point, Edward becomes anxious and distressed, asking her how will it manage to come out.

There was no doubt that Mrs E had finally seen the link between Edward's play with the trains, the story he asked her to read, his reaction to the story, and the trouble he had with allowing his stools to come out of his body. Mrs E looked relieved, and Edward was clearly pleased with finding that his game had been translated into words. Mrs E wanted to stay on the safe side, and, in spite of her understanding, she still requested a definite plan to put into practice. We discussed making a chart of Edward's progress—and his success would lead to his getting "a metal ball" that he was keen to have. I emphasized that it was important not to ask Edward about going to the toilet, but, rather, to take him there at the same time each day, so that his body could develop its own rhythm of functioning.

Mrs E did not wish to make another appointment at that point, and we arranged that she would let me know of Edward's progress. Two months later, Mrs E reported that Edward had now developed a regular rhythm where he defecated every second day, without requiring any drugs. To my surprise, she added that he was still occasionally wetting his bed, something I had not been told before. I urged Mrs E to attend again, but she refused this, saying that "Edward would just grow out of it" in due course. I had to accept that Mrs E could not appreciate that Edward might be as much distressed by his enuresis as he had been about his constipation. Prognostically speaking, this did not augur too well for Edward's development, but it was just possible that he might manage to achieve bladder control even if without the support of his parents.

Comment

Mrs E did not consult the paediatrician again, but I heard from the GP that Edward seemed to have maintained control of his bowel movements. The consultation had shown that Edward had found in his play a language whereby he could express the nature of his unconscious anxieties, but it was sad that his mother seemed unable to recognize how valuable this capacity of his was. Like the mother of the child described next, Mrs E was also quite unable to accept any other than verbal expressions of the child's thoughts and feelings. I suspect that this may be a very important factor in what Winnicott called "the false self" (1960), where the child adapts to the mother's capacities and learns that certain feelings can only be expressed through symptoms or behaviour or not at all.

Edward is a wonderful example of how a child seems to come for a consultation as if with his homework prepared. I do believe that this occurs very often indeed, but that it is not that easy for the consultant to pick up the cues given by the child. The only guideline I follow results from my conviction that the child wants to get rid of his problem and looks to this stranger as a potential helper— and then it becomes a matter of looking for cues that might relate to the symptom, as it is perceived by the child. This is the only explanation I can find for my, for example, taking Edward's banging of his toys with increasing excitement as a rendering of the noise that his stools might make, a mixture of excitement and fear.

I failed to understand how Mrs E could help Edward overcome his phobia of defecating and then refuse to attempt a similar approach regarding his wetting. This could well be due to her objecting to my technique, but it could also result from her difficulty in seeing Edward gaining further independence from her ministrations. Unfortunately, I had no opportunity of exploring these possibilities.

Jane

Jane's story is a rich illustration of the ways in which a child uses physical complaints to convey distress to the parents. Psychoanalytic theory speaks of fixations to points of conflict and of exaggerated cathexis of body parts, but a case like Jane's presents important evidence to show that the physical symptomatology constitutes, first and foremost, a language learnt from the parents. A child will "learn" which language his parents can grasp and respond to: if the parent only reacts to physical complaints, these will multiply. Indeed, the particular choice of organ may have a specific meaning for the child, and, therefore, this should be looked into; however, we must not lose sight of the purpose served by the symptom within the child's relationship to the parents.

Jane was a very intelligent and articulate 8-year-old who attended a highly academic school, where she always achieved good results. She was seen as a shy and sensitive girl, but she had many friends and all teachers were fond of her. Suddenly, she began to complain of troublesome headaches, and this led to her being "placed somewhere quiet until she felt better". The GP was consulted after this had gone on for about four months. In his letter to the paediatrician, he mentioned that Jane now also complained of "a curious sensation in the head that appears about once each week and lasts for a few minutes each time". This was "a sensation of a shower of rain or light passing up through her head and during this time she is unable to concentrate and needs to sit quietly". The GP had found no abnormality in his examination, but he wondered whether Jane might have "a migrainous condition or even some sort of curious epileptiform phenomenon".

Jane had a skull X-ray and an E.E.G.: both gave normal results. The paediatrician explored in depth Jane's account of her symptoms and also learnt of recent family events that had affected Jane's life. Her conclusion was that she could find no evidence of organic pathology and, while being prepared to request ophthalmological and neurological assessments, felt that a psychiatric evaluation should be undertaken first. Fortunately, Jane's mother, Mrs J, agreed to this, and they were referred to me.

Jane and Mrs J formed a very attractive pair. Mrs J was young, attractive, well dressed and self-possessed; Jane was pretty and immaculately turned out, though shy and reserved. Jane was able to tell me about her symptoms, particularly her "funny feelings": detailed descriptions of noises, lights, and mainly water coming up her head whenever she looked into slits, holes, or certain illuminated surfaces.

The referring doctors had described most of these symptoms, and both Jane and her mother had obviously gone through this account many times before. Jane spoke calmly, but there was no doubt that she was frightened by her experiences, and I noticed that Mrs J's comments indicated fear of whatever illness might be causing them. I asked Jane about life at home and at school, and I soon found myself thoroughly confused with names and relationships. It was obvious that Jane and her mother were quite used to such a reaction, and they laughed warmly about my muddle, promptly setting out to help me to understand the complexity of their family structure. Jane's father had left the family but had kept in touch with them. He now had a child from another marriage. Mrs J had now married a man who had children from a previous marriage.

Mrs J told me that her new husband had been quite involved with the family life for a long time, even though they had only married some seven months previously. But I noticed that Jane dated this marriage as "four months ago", a date that corresponded to the period of time when her symptoms had appeared. It was very striking that both male and female members of the family network were eminently successful people in their chosen fields of work. Mrs J herself worked as a high-powered administrator, and over the years she had achieved considerable success in the various areas to which she had turned. She had an impressive command of language, and, to judge from how easily she made herself comfortable talking to me, she was clearly very able to make contact with people.

As Jane was telling me about her daily life and the transition from home to school environments, she suddenly mentioned, quite in passing, that she was enuretic. I was taken by surprise, since there had been no reference to this in the correspondence I had received from the GP and from the consultant paediatrician. It was not just the question of Jane's age; she was clearly a girl who took great pride in her physical appearance, and I could only imagine that she would feel deeply ashamed about wetting her bed. But I was even more surprised by Mrs J's reaction to her daughter's revelation: at first, she just laughed, but then she put into words the fact that she could not see why I attached any importance to this subject of bedwetting.

It would be difficult to reconstruct the discussion that took place at this point of the interview. Jane must have known that her mother's views about the occurrence and significance of the wetting were at variance with her own. Her embarrassment was acute; she was visibly struggling, caught between her wish to tell me about the wetting and the obviously long-standing awareness of her mother's incapacity to accept her account of her feelings—at least, about this particular experience.

Mrs J tried to put the record straight by telling me that "as a matter of fact Jane has not wet her bed in a long time". Jane meekly stated that she had done so even the previous night. Mrs J was astonished, and it was some time before they sorted out how it was that both of them were correct in their statements. It emerged that the morning starts for Jane with her nanny coming into the room (I had not known there was such a person in the house), and Jane reported how, if she has wet her bed during the night, she will say a plaintive "sorry" to the nanny. It is the nanny who takes charge of changing the bedclothes, and Jane is acutely aware of her fear that the nanny will report the wetting to her mother. But before the nanny's appearance, Jane will already have gone through a private ordeal. She described with obvious shame how she wakes up as soon as she wets herself; she gets out of bed, goes to the bathroom, where she undresses, washes, and dries herself, before returning to bed, where she puts the towel between herself and the sheet.

But the family had, apparently, developed a routine that explained how Jane and her mother managed to hold on to the stories that each one had created. Whatever happens in the night, once Jane has washed and got ready for the day, she dresses and then goes to the kitchen and makes a cup of tea, which she lovingly takes to her mother in bed—so, from Mrs J's point of view, there had been no wetting in a long time. Mrs J was quite shaken when she heard this account.

But no sooner was the incidence of the wetting sorted out, I found that a new disagreement/misunderstanding developed—now, over its significance. Mrs J told us that when she had spoken to her own mother about Jane's wetting, she had reminded Mrs J that she had wet her bed until she was 10 years old. She was laughing when recounting this, and I indicated my puzzlement. I asked her if she had any memories about the wetting itself or whether this was something she was prepared to accept as a correct story from her mother. No, she did not have clear memories about the event or how often it happened, but she did remember quite vividly the feeling of pleasure, "the wet enveloping you, so very nice—true, the next morning it felt awful, but . . .".

Jane burst in with an uncontrolled "It is *horrid!*" that surprised both me and Mrs J. The way in which Mrs J went on speaking about Jane's reaction made me think that, somehow, Mrs J had taken her expression of violent objection to represent Jane's agreement with her views—that is, that the "awfulness" lay in the wetting becoming known to others. I looked at Jane and asked her if I had understood her mother correctly and whether this interpretation was correct. She hesitated before muttering a "Yes", confirming that she agreed with her mother.

I said I was surprised because I felt that Jane's account of how disturbed she was by the wetting and how she dealt with this during the night would suggest that it was the *experience* of wetting herself and lying in the wet clothes that produced strong feelings in her. Mrs J promptly indicated her disagreement with my interpretation and turned to Jane, asking her to tell us what she thought of what I had said. Jane lowered her head and obviously struggled before she managed to say, quietly, "He is right".

Both Jane and her mother were disturbed by this unexpected sequence and the appearance of a conflict in which Jane's loyalty was put to the test. I tried to explain the reason for my pursuing what I had thought was a disagreement: it was quite natural for Mrs J to interpret Jane's reaction to the wetting along the lines of what had been her own experience, but unless Jane managed to make her mother aware of what she herself went through, Mrs J could not but conclude that her understanding was correct—and Jane would remain under the belief that her mother expected her to profess agreement with this reading of her emotional experience, even though it did not, in fact, match her own feelings about it. I did not expand on the implications of this overt compliance, although, from what I had been told about Jane's life in her extended family, it seemed to be an important factor in Jane's attitude towards the adults around her.

At this point, I suggested that Jane made a drawing. I was hoping that this might give us further insight into Jane's feelings, and I would also have the opportunity of talking to Mrs J about the environment in which Jane had grown up. Indeed, Mrs J was quite happy to explain in more detail the many changes that had characterized Jane's home life. Formal relationships had been formed and dissolved, but Mrs J seemed quite sure that a good atmosphere had always prevailed and that all the adults had consistently sustained not just civilized attitudes to each other, but also friendly and supportive ones. I thought that she might consider it conceivable that Jane could have harboured feelings of unhappiness, disappointment, or resentment, but this was obviously a hypothesis that she would never, in practice, accept as a possibility.

I do not think it necessary to repeat here all the information I obtained from Mrs J, as it is not really relevant to understanding what followed. I had noticed that Jane had started to draw something but had then turned the page around before drawing the picture that she eventually showed us. She said that "the tree had gone wrong" and she had, therefore, started the picture again.

On the left of the tree (Figure 3.4), a mother and daughter are standing together. Their arms are raised "because that is how I like to draw people". An aunt is on the other side, holding a basket where a bird is going to fall; the radio is switched on and there is

Figure 3.4

noise coming out of it. I asked why the bird was falling and what would happen to it, but Jane explained that she did not know why this was so. "Wee" is the rendering of the noise of the bird falling. Mrs J thought she should pre-empt any further Freudian extrapolations and explained that the family word for urine is "pee", not wee. Unexpectedly, Mrs J said that the tree in the picture looked like the one they have in their garden, and Jane confirmed this, clearly pleased that her mother had identified that element of her drawing.

Looking more carefully at the picture, I noticed that the little girl's hand is very near a stain between the mother's legs, but I decided not to mention this. I also wondered if there was a connection between the raised hands and a denial of contact between hands and genitals, but again I left this unspoken. Instead, I called their attention to my impression that the bird would fall not into the basket but, rather, would hit the aunt on the head. Jane burst out laughing, quite amused at this idea. Mrs J attempted a smile, but I thought she had now become rather impatient with what interpretations I put on my "discoveries".

In fact, I did not enlarge on my comment. We had now been together for over an hour and a half, and I thought we should bring the interview to a close. I suggested a second meeting and tried to make explicit a couple of points from our discussion. I suggested that Jane kept a record of significant events in the following two weeks, when we would meet again, so that we could explore any possible correlation with her wetting. I mentioned, as if in passing, that there might be some connection between the "water coming up the head" and the problem of wetting, but I mostly stressed that I believed that her symptoms were her way of trying to convey her feelings to her mother—and unless she found a way of articulating these feelings clearly, her mother would remain unable to understand her. I did not put into words the corresponding need for her mother to be prepared to *listen* to what Jane might want to say, but I hoped that Mrs J was able to infer this from the course of the interview.

When I met Jane and her mother two weeks later, they were pleased to report that Jane had not wet her bed since our interview. Jane was clearly proud of this. Mrs J had picked up my cue and she had spent considerable time speaking to Jane and trying to learn of her feelings—but, very much in passing, I was told of a development that I could never guess was possible.

As we were talking, Jane had picked up some sheets of paper and she drew two girls: one wearing glasses and the other not. Jane commented that she wanted to use glasses and added that her brother wants to use braces. Mrs J laughed, saying that "they obviously think this is fashionable". She went on to tell me that she had taken Jane to an ophthalmologist. I assumed that this was a long-standing appointment and Jane's remark probably meant that some glasses had been prescribed, but it would not occur to me to see any connection between this information and what knowledge I had gained of Jane and her needs up to that point. I was not prepared, therefore, for Mrs J telling me why she had decided to have Jane's eyes tested: when I pointed out during our first meeting that the bird in Jane's picture would fall on the woman's head, rather than fall into the basket as Jane had meant to depict the scene, Mrs J remembered that Jane occasionally has trouble in reading and she concluded that there must be something wrong with her sight!

Jane explained that the girl without glasses does not want to have any, whilst the other one likes to have them—"no, actually she does not want them . . . but does not mind them". I found it quite painful to watch Jane using her picture to indicate her own efforts to present a façade of acceptance of something she clearly did not like or want to have to do, when all the time her mother was unable to see any connection between the comments on the drawing and Jane's own feelings. Mrs J made it quite plain that Jane was simply telling me the story of two girls in a picture.

I put into words my impression that Jane seemed to find it very difficult to voice any feelings of opposition against what she takes as the adults' expectations of her. I asked Jane if she could imagine herself actually saying "No, I do not want". She lifted her shoulders, bowed her head, and muttered, "Not really . . .". Mrs J said that there were many times when it was quite impossible to get Jane to do something she felt it was important for her to do. I thought that if Jane saw herself as incapable of being openly defiant, even if this was no more than ordinary self-assertion, her mother was determined to describe her as self-confident and, at times, stubborn. I wondered whether perhaps Mrs J thought I was trying to provoke Jane into conforming with my own idea of herself, but I decided to let the matter rest in case we ended up putting Jane into a situation where she might feel stuck in a conflict of loyalties.

We arranged a further appointment for three weeks later.

Our third meeting brought a mixture of good, positive developments and a sad warning that whatever progress we managed to make in our meetings might not be built upon. Jane's difficulty in making open, explicit statements of her needs and wishes seemed to persist, and her symptoms appeared to be the only "acceptable" language in which to convey her sense of disappointment or disillusionment. Mrs J, on the other hand, had made a determined effort to come closer to Jane, but she still retained an intense disbelief that this closeness might be in any way related to the progress made by Jane in overcoming her various symptoms.

Both Jane and her mother seemed in great spirits. The headaches and "funny feelings" had disappeared and she had coped extremely well with the last weeks of term at school. She had done very well in her examinations and the teachers had commented that she appeared a much happier child. At home, the picture was similar, and Mrs J was pleased with Jane's progress. A negative note was the fact that Jane had wet her bed three nights over the preceding week, an event that upset Jane, particularly as she could not understand why this symptom had recurred.

Mrs J was extremely proud of how much she had talked to Jane. She felt that this was a remarkable discovery, the more surprising when she had never been aware of keeping any distance between herself and her much loved daughter. She recounted with pleasure how she had reported her "discovery" to many members of the family, with all the pride that goes with a newly found skill. Against this background, it was disconcerting to hear Mrs J saying that Jane had probably wet her bed because her brother had come back from boarding-school or—who knows?—it might have been because her school term had come to an end and, as she now slept later than usual, this could lead to her sleeping far too deep and not noticing when she wanted to pee.

Jane told me about her plans for the holidays. She was to spend some time with grandmother and then stay with her father abroad, after which she would join her mother for the last stretch of the holiday. Without any warning, she began to cry. No sobs or visible movements, just sad, silent tears that rolled down her cheeks, whilst Jane looked immensely helpless. I indicated my surprise and Mrs J spoke words of sympathy, but Jane was at a loss to explain why she was crying at this point.

As the silence persisted, I suggested that Jane should make some drawing, whilst I continued speaking to her mother. I was hoping that her picture might help us to understand the reason for her tears.

Jane concentrated in her drawing, though it was clear that she was following my conversation with her mother. I find it difficult to reproduce the nuances of the dialogue that followed. Mrs J was a sensitive, loving, extremely articulate young woman, whose life and especially her work must have brought her into contact with innumerable people in distress. She was living in an age where it has been impossible not to read and to hear of the link between emotions and body symptoms—and yet, having just described Jane's progress and her own efforts to achieve this result, here was Mrs J putting forward hypotheses that failed to take this into account. I have quoted above two of these, but as our conversation moved on and we considered again how the wetting had stopped, Mrs J commented: "I suppose it was some physical failure that came right, after all . . .".

This was not the first time that I found this puzzling attitude of disbelief regarding a child's overcoming bedwetting. Mrs J's interpretation of Jane's improvement indicated her doubt that this was a permanent achievement. This is only too commonly found with a parent who struggled with a sphincter dysfunction in his or her own childhood. Such parents start off by assuming that the child's symptom is "the same thing" that they had in their childhood, which leads them to expect that the child will only overcome it at the same point as they got rid of their problem. However, these parents invariably convey a sense that they had nothing to do with the cessation of their dysfunction; each person weaves his or her own rationalization to explain why the wetting (or the messing) disappeared one day, but the underlying layer is one of total helplessness: pain, distress, shame while the symptom persisted, and relief once it disappeared. Sadly, when seen as adults, they will seldom admit to these affects—instead, they recount various face-saving manoeuvres they used so as to disguise the problem, but these hardly disguise the experience of being saved by a miracle and then living for a long time under the fear that the symptom might return.

When their child overcomes the sphincter dysfunction following a therapeutic intervention, these parents can feel very disturbed. One of the parents I saw kept repeating, with great anguish, the accusation that her mother had not sought "the right help". And when a child improves, as Jane did, thanks to a parent understanding the child's needs, there is the danger that this parent feels guilty for not having spotted earlier what these needs were.

I felt that Mrs J was struggling with feelings like these. She must have sensed that Jane was using her physical symptoms to bring about some closeness with her, but her need to sort out her feelings about her own past and for her earlier approach to Jane probably made it impossible for her to abandon her views that the wetting, the headaches, and all the "funny feelings" had some organic underlying cause.

Jane indicated that she had finished her drawing (Figure 3.5), and I asked her to describe it to us. The sun and clouds are drawn in yellow. Under the water, a fish is going to eat a tadpole that is running away and then proceeds to eat the other tadpole that is eating some reeds; some frogspawn float further away. Jane did not know why she had drawn this scene, and she shrugged her shoulders in silence at several questions we put to her. Mrs J praised her warmly, saying it was "a very nice picture!"

Figure 3.5

I decided to ignore who was eating whom or what projections were depicted in this "destructive", "oral sadistic" scene. Instead, I voiced my impression that it might be significant that the light and beauty prevailing above water gave no clue to what was going on underneath. Mrs J burst out laughing, perhaps more kindly than friendly: "Oh, come!, that is all to do with what they have learnt at school!"

I decided to try again with my reading of the picture and said that "I believe the picture might be a reflection of what Jane feels and the explanation for her crying: she may find it difficult to keep bright and sunny, while keeping to herself all the turmoil underneath". Mrs J turned to Jane and asked, "Do you think he is right?", and Jane nodded, again crying in silence. Mrs J was dumbfounded.

I thought that I should make some connection between this sense of failed communication and the previous efforts that had brought them together, so I said: "I do not pretend to know what exactly *caused* the wetting, but I do believe it stopped because you (*addressing Mrs J*) came closer to Jane, as you described. It may well be that your telling the family about it made Jane fear that you might feel you had talked enough. Plus the coming holidays, where apparently Jane will spend long periods with other relations, may have heightened her fear of losing you again." Mrs J could not see much sense in this, but she turned to Jane, "Could that really be so?", and again Jane nodded her head.

It was clear that it would be some time before we met again, if at all. I carefully pointed out to Mrs J that, however gratifying it was to see Jane get rid of her physical symptoms, I felt they should bear in mind the possibility of her having some individual psychotherapy at a later point. Jane was clearly a very sensitive child, and she might need further help to improve her self-confidence. Mrs J barely disguised her reluctance in contemplating such a plan—but we left it that they would let me know how Jane was getting on after the holidays and her new term at school.

When I heard from Mrs J, she reported that "Jane seems to be much more relaxed than she was some months ago and she is certainly much more able to confide her worries to me". The bedwetting "is virtually non-existent" and if it happens that something brings on "the funny feeling" (she quoted the example of "a plate of fried, mashed potato slightly burnt at the edges"), Jane reports it "with an apologetic smile" and makes it clear that the sensation does not persist for any length of time. Mrs J added that Jane "still remains a sensitive little girl who cannot bear ever to be second-best at home or at school: it worries her a lot", and she went on to quote Jane's occasional reaction of distress at the possibility of being displaced by a sibling in her parents' love.

I thought that Mrs J's letter conveyed very clearly her feeling that there was now a close relationship between Jane and herself which allowed her to help Jane whenever this was necessary. She assured me that she would take my advice if I felt that psychotherapy was still necessary, but I wrote back to confirm my support for the changes that she had implemented. I would be happy to see Jane again, but only if and when she and/or her mother wished me to do so.

Comment

My decision not to urge Mrs J to let Jane have psychotherapy was determined by my impression that such a recommendation might be seen by Mrs J as a statement of my doubt about her reliability as a helper. I must confess that I was, indeed, uncertain that Mrs J would sustain her attitude of interest and closeness with Jane, but on balance I decided to take a stance that might lead Mrs J to feel that I trusted her capacity to continue to help Jane.

I did obtain some follow-up information on Jane, but only over a few months. The GP told me that he had not been consulted further for symptoms similar to the original ones, and I did not hear from the family again. My impression is that Jane would experience problems on reaching adolescence, since her difficulty with self-assertion and her basically unconfident self-image would point to a considerable need for external support—and, considering the extremely complex family circumstances around her, this might not correspond to her need for self-discovery.

I found Jane's a very painful case. Lack of parental support is usually associated with lack of sophistication, poverty of material conditions, or extreme personal conflicts in the parents that impede them from recognizing the child's needs. None of these were in clear evidence in Jane's background. Quite the opposite—Mrs J was genuinely caring and willing to help her daughter, but her attitude to "feelings" appeared to lead her to a serious blindness regarding Jane's emotional experiences. It is conceivable that Mrs J had other personal problems which were not recognized in my interviews, but from our meetings I could only accept that Mrs J was not prepared to look at Jane's problems as any other than physical events. Linked to this would be the fact that she seemed to believe that Jane's need for closeness could be satisfied by any adult who happened to make him/herself available.

This is a case where, sadly, I would say that the interviews were extremely useful and helpful—but this help might not be as lasting as it might or should be, because of Jane's emotional dependence on her mother, who was unable to give Jane the further help she desperately wanted and needed.

CHAPTER FOUR

Mainly the child

It can be difficult to evaluate the precise role that some parents play in the joint interview. The three children in this chapter were chosen because of the rich meanings conveyed in their drawings, but it is interesting to note how differently their parents reacted to the interview and to the child's participation.

"Georgia's" mother followed with great attention each step of the interview, and her participation was effective and timely. Georgia felt protected by her mother, and she often checked how attentive her mother was to my questions, as if needing her permission to answer them. Someone might hypothesize that I was seen as a potential attacker, much as the circumstances—an attack by a dog—that had brought her to the interview. Mrs G was immensely at ease and appeared content to follow Georgia's cues. However interested Mrs G was, the most important elements of the consultation came from Georgia's drawings. As will be seen, these are an example of the superimposed pictures described in chapter two. Looking at the superimposed image, Georgia could understand immediately why the dog's attack had produced such traumatic effects on her. It seems that seeing what her unconscious had made of the experience was sufficient for her nightmares and fears to disappear.

Contrary to Georgia's case, "Harriet's" case is quite painful because of its prognosis. Harriet produced fascinating pictures, and these give a dramatic view of her feelings. However, her mother was too caught up with serious pathology of her own, and the prognosis for Harriet's development has to be very guarded indeed. I tried hard to persuade Mrs H to allow Harriet to have individual psychotherapy, but she refused this; in any case, even if she had accepted it, such individual work had little chance of being sufficient to counterbalance the pressure of conflicts that Harriet lived under. It is conceivable that she might find her way to psychotherapy in her adolescence, and this might well prove an effective option.

"Leon" is another case of sphincter dysfunction, but his drawings show quite poignantly the change from the studied, almost contrived, drawing, to progressively more regressed pictures, where conscious control is gradually suspended and the unconscious picture that summarizes the pathogenic fantasy is represented on paper. Watching this experience, one can recognize that the words articulating the interpretation are almost unnecessary, since the child can immediately perceive what had been frightening him. Leon's parents were very involved with him and were clearly interested in his thoughts and feelings, but Leon's anxieties about his defecation had totally escaped them, since they had an easy-going attitude to life in general and to the upbringing of children. It was quite amusing to hear, once again, parents confirming a child's question that "children are born from the underneath of the body", with no awareness of what images the child constructs on those words. In my experience, this is an extremely common occurrence.

Georgia

Georgia had been attacked by a dog when she went with friends to a fun fair and, at some point, decided to choose a shortcut while trying to get to another part of the fair. They were passing behind one of the stalls when they suddenly found themselves confronted by the dog, which jumped on them and happened to bite Georgia's lower lip.

Georgia was intensely disturbed by this experience, but what eventually brought her to a child psychiatrist was the fact that for the ensuing two months she kept waking up at night, screaming and crying inconsolably, referring to ghastly nightmares that she was unable to remember and, at times, also having episodes of sleep-walking. They consulted the family doctor, who advised seeing me at the local child guidance clinic.

Georgia, an attractive and intelligent 12-year-old, came to the consultation with her mother, Mrs G. Georgia told me about her family and school life. Mrs G was happy to clarify any points about the family life that Georgia was not too sure of and to answer my questions. Mrs G looked much younger than her mid-30s age, and she had an easy-going, friendly, and close relationship with Georgia, who was one of three children. Mr G had left the family some years earlier and now lived abroad, but they had kept a close enough relationship that enabled the children to move easily and confidently from one to the other parent. Mrs G held a senior administrative position in a commercial firm and was very involved with the education and general upbringing of her children.

Georgia told me of friends at school and in the neighbourhood; she saw herself as a successful, popular member of her circle of friends and colleagues. Her comments about her parents and other members of the family seemed reasonable and well balanced. I gradually came to the conclusion that Georgia's nightmares were to be understood within the context of the attack she had suffered: whatever unconscious conflicts she might have as a result of family experiences did not seem to have much relevance to the present crisis.

I asked Georgia to tell me the story of the attack in detail. She answered my questions, but time and again she indicated her puzzlement as to why I insisted she should try to remember the details of each step she had taken that evening. I explained that the fact that the nightmares were still haunting her indicated that some element of her experience that evening must have taken on some particular meaning that she had not succeeded in working out in all her attempts at discovering what had happened to her. She could see the logic of my words, but several times she tried to dismiss some question either because she could not remember what happened or because she thought it could not be important. I was fortunate in that Mrs G agreed with my argument and repeatedly encouraged Georgia to try harder to answer my questions, which she did.

Georgia and her friend had met other school and neighbourhood friends at the fair. They had rides on various machines and ate the usual range of fast foods that youngsters relish at fairs. At one point, Georgia and her friend decided to have a particular brand of ice-cream but knew they would have to walk a long way to reach the stall that sold it. They told their friends of their intention and moved away from the group. As they checked their bearings, they realized that they could reduce the distance by walking behind some stalls, rather than along the main walkways. Georgia remembered that they had considered the possibility that there might be danger in taking that shortcut, but "danger" was used as an umbrella word—they did not discuss what might be involved.

Georgia told me that as they were walking behind one of the stalls, they suddenly saw a huge dog lying on the ground. For a moment, they stood still, thinking what to do and trying to convince themselves that the dog might remain quiet. But unexpectedly the dog took a short run and jumped on them. Georgia could remember the dog hitting her and throwing her on the ground, but then there was a blank and the next thing she could remember was being at home, with her mother and sisters crying for her.

After some more questions, I had to admit that Georgia had told me everything that she could remember. She had no recollection of her nightmares, except for those dreams in which the attack was being repeated, but even these would stop precisely at the same point where her recollections stopped. Her mother commented that she had tried many times to help Georgia to remember her movements that evening. As a matter of fact, Georgia's friend had told Georgia and her mother that, when both of them began to cry and scream, many people had come rushing to find out what had happened. They had helped Georgia to get up, and when they saw that she was bleeding, she was taken to the first-aid tent in the fair and, from there, to the casualty department of the local hospital. But Georgia knew all this as information given to her, which was not available to her memory.

We had reached an impasse. Considering the age of the girls and the notion of "danger" they were daring to face, it would not be difficult to suppose that there was a sexual content to Georgia's anxieties. I was, however, loath to voice such a hypothesis without having some cue that Georgia might recognize as coming from herself. Just to present her with a sexual interpretation "out of nowhere" (from her perspective), might lead her to associate it with the experience of the dog jumping on her. I decided, therefore, to try an alternative approach.

I explained to Georgia that sometimes one can reach a lost memory through the use of drawings. Predictably, she looked baffled, suspicious, and embarrassed, but she agreed to give it a try. Normally, in similar consultations, I am careful not to make suggestions to the child, leaving it to the child to choose what to draw, and I also ask parents not to give ideas or make requests at that point. The rationale is easy to recognize: firstly, we are counting on the child's unconscious to bring to the fore something relevant that will help us to understand the child; but secondly, and equally important, this leaves the child to consider the drawing as his own spontaneous production. Here, however, we had a special situation. I had asked endless questions focusing on one single sequence in Georgia's life, and, even if it could be argued that free drawings might still lead her to express relevant features of the traumatic experience, I decided to depart from my usual technique. I asked Georgia to draw a picture of her meeting the dog.

Georgia's first drawing (Figure 4.1) shows her together with her friend walking towards the part of the stall where the dog was. I noticed the expression on the dog's face, and this did not seem to me particularly fierce (some dog lovers who saw this drawing commented that this was a very sensitive picture of a large and lovable dog), but I made no comment. I asked Georgia to draw what happened next.

Her second drawing (Figure 4.2) shows the dog biting Georgia's lips and drops of blood falling on the ground. Her friend is further back, with an expression of horror on her face. After considering this picture for a while, I asked her to draw what she thought

Figure 4.1

Figure 4.2

had happened next. She hesitated briefly and drew herself on the ground with the dog on top of her (Figure 4.3), but she decided that this was "wrong" and crossed it out. She repeated the same scene a few inches above the wrong image and I noticed that in this picture the dog is entirely beside her body, whilst in the first one it was placed between her legs, but I said nothing. When I asked what had then happened, she wrote "Blanck" to indicate the gap in her memory, but then went on to draw herself crying and bleeding, already at home, with her mother and sisters staring at her in horror.

By now, I was quite convinced that Georgia had built a sexual fantasy over the attack by the dog, but I had to find a way of conveying this interpretation to her in a manner that might make sense to her. I asked her to go back to the earlier part of her account where she had spoken of "danger". She denied that she had any idea of what kind of danger she and her friends had in mind. It was impossible to know whether this was a true statement or whether she felt ashamed in front of her mother or myself. A further compli-cation was that she might be trying to guess what answer I wanted

Figure 4.3

from her and, anyway, it was difficult to frame any question without loading it in some direction. Mrs G was following this dialogue without saying anything. I explained my difficulty in wanting, without influencing her, to help Georgia to identify what might have been on her mind, and, finally, mimicking a tone of voice that might sound like her mother's, I said "Please make sure that you do not move away from your friends! Mind you don't go into dark places and definitely not away from the main paths! You just have to be careful in case you find . . ." and I stopped.

Mrs G smiled. She had now recognized what I had in mind, and I think she did give Georgia some cue, because Georgia soon muttered, very quietly, "some man . . ." Mrs G smiled and confirmed that this was a warning that she issued very forcibly each time Georgia went out with her friends to the park, particularly if there was a fair going on. I asked Georgia what danger did men pose, but she kept silent. Mrs G obliged at this point and made explicit that her warning had included explaining to Georgia about sexual attacks and how to defend herself from this.

I went back to the drawings and called Georgia's attention to her "wrong" drawing. I explained to her my idea of putting two drawings on top of each other, as if they had been made as a single picture. I showed her that I was not just making pictures fit, but that the corners of the page corresponded to each other. I lifted the two drawings (Figures 4.2 and 4.3), put them exactly on each other (Figure 4.4), and asked her if she saw anything that struck her as interesting or significant.

Georgia laughed, clearly embarrassed, and said that the dog was now totally on top of her. I explained to her that she *knew* that she had been attacked by a dog that had bitten her lip, but the pictures showed that "deep in her mind" (or words to this effect) she had remembered the warnings about men who could attack her and subject her to a sexual assault—and she had put the two together, so that she was now reacting as if she had been sexually attacked.

Mrs G voiced surprise but commented that "it made sense". She was fascinated by my picking up my interpretation in the drawings and asked questions about this. Georgia was visibly relaxed, but looked thoughtful. We agreed to meet again two weeks later, to check on progress.

Figure 4.4

On the morning of the appointment, Mrs G telephoned the clinic: Georgia was in bed with flu, but she had told her mother that she did not, really, want to see me again. Mrs G added that she was inclined to agree with Georgia, since the nightmares had ceased. Right from the day we had met, Georgia had slept through the nights, and there was, therefore, no reason to see me again. I spotted a thought going through my mind that here they were deciding "to let sleeping dogs lie" . . .

Comment

Nowadays, Georgia would be diagnosed as showing a "post-traumatic stress reaction", and this account shows one way in which such cases can be approached. But should one see these cases as self-limited, or is it more prudent to investigate some pathological substratum that made such intense reactions possible? Theoretically, some would argue for the latter course of action, but this idea stems from the theory of overdetermination, where one's reactions to external stimuli are seen as influenced, if not caused, by earlier experiences. In fact, most proponents of this theory will see ever earlier experiences as the ones that are relevant, and in practice these professionals claim that it is the earliest infantile unconscious fantasies that are the "real" causes of later pathological behaviour.

I do not subscribe to this theory, mainly because it is self-fulfilling. Any material will be interpreted in line with the analyst's frame of reference, and caution is required when the evidence to confirm or refute our opinion is, itself, liable to be read within the same conceptual framework on which the theory is based. In other words, all we have to substantiate our hypotheses about "earliest experiences" is the information that will be gained from the same patient under discussion, which puts us in a circular chain of data and hypotheses.

From a pragmatic point of view, the situation is very different. In the present case, Georgia refused to attend for one follow-up appointment, which suggests that she would not embark on any long-term exploration of her life experiences. Would I then be accused of "curing her too quickly"? This is a question that only others can answer. Because I saw Georgia as a normally developing youngster, I felt quite pleased that I had helped her to overcome a crisis. Follow-up information from the family doctor was that Georgia had not presented further difficulties, and I think that this supports my approach to the case.

Harriet

I saw Harriet when she was 6 years old, and, though our meeting was illuminating and helped her to overcome her presenting problem, she went on to experience quite a series of other difficulties. Sadly, Harriet's mother, Mrs H, struggled with enormously complex problems of her own, and we never managed to offer effective long-term help to either of them.

Harriet was seen by a clinical psychologist over several months. For over one year Harriet had been constipated for periods of up to a fortnight. She had been admitted a few times to the paediatric

ward of the (district general) hospital, where appropriate intervention would lead to emptying of the bowels and a resumption of
some more normal rhythm of defecation. However, as soon as
Harriet was discharged, problems appeared again, and eventually
admission to hospital had to be resorted to. The psychologist tried
to teach Harriet and her mother different techniques based on
behavioural lines, but these invariably proved ineffective. Eventually, the psychologist decided to refer them to me, hoping they
might respond to some insight-based approach.

Harriet was beautifully turned out. She was shy and looked
fearful when we first met, but she quickly relaxed and made
herself at home. Mrs H was at home from the first moment we
met, smiling in a warm, spontaneous way, as if we had known
each other for a long time. No doubt, this would make it easier for
Harriet to relax, but only gradually did I discover that Mrs H's
attitude of familiarity was also responsible for Harriet's initial fear-
fulness. No sooner had I introduced myself to Harriet, and explained the kind of work I practised, than she declared that she had
already overcome her problems and was sure that I would confirm
that she did not need any further treatment.

The psychologist had accepted my invitation to join us for this
consultation, and she now asked Harriet how it had come about
that her problems were gone. Harriet said she had been going to
the toilet regularly, and, anyway, she had been dreading coming to
see me. Harriet was intelligent enough to perceive that this might
be misinterpreted, so she added that these feelings were not related
to me, personally, but had to do with the fact that she hated hospitals, and she wished I would dismiss her before long. We all smiled
at her tact, and we tried to reassure her that this visit would be
different from any others, since I would not do anything invasive
or hurtful: I only wanted to talk. Harriet accepted this reassurance,
because she seemed to relax and answered my questions.

Harriet told me about her school life. She had many friends and
felt she was quite popular among them. Her teachers seemed to be
fond of her. Harriet spoke with some sadness about the number of
times she had to miss school due to her visits and admissions to
hospital, but because hospital, home, and school were all in the
same neighbourhood, her friends kept in touch with her. She said
home life was very happy, and she told me about her recently born

sibling. The baby was 4 months old, and Harriet described her with tones of pleasure and admiration. Mrs H commented how she had feared Harriet might resent the birth of the baby, but in fact she was proving to be "very mature" and always happy to help.

I asked Mrs H about her own life. She came from a large family. The oldest sibling had died from leukaemia, but the others were all healthy. Mrs H laughed when she told me of her problems with feeding. She had gone through periods where she became quite obsessed with eating, and this meant putting on a lot of weight, which then led her to endless consultations in search of medical help. She had been quite successful at school and described herself as equally proficient in her professional life. Her husband had immigrated to England some years earlier. He was an only child and was clearly pleased to be away from his family of origin. The couple discovered a talent for business and had created their own small enterprise, which gave sufficient profit for them to lead a comfortable life.

As usual in cases of children with bowel problems, I inquired about the parents' toilet routines. It turned out that *both* grand-mothers believed that constipation constitutes a poisoning of the body. Not only this, but Mr H's mother took this belief to a dra-matic conclusion: Mrs H mimicked the mother-in-law, telling us that "come 9 a.m., she would look at the watch and if he had not been to the toilet, he either had to produce stools immediately or else he was given an enema!" It would, therefore, not be surprising to be told that both Mr and Mrs H had no fixed routine about their bowel habits. But Mrs H burst out laughing; she did not mock me or anybody else who believed in fixed times for anything, but she wanted us to know how delighted she and her husband were that there was no certain, established time for *anything* at all in their home. No timetables—and this held for mealtimes, bedtimes, or anything else.

Harriet surprised us at this point, suddenly chipping in to her mother that she wished mother was available at breakfast time. She added that her father would go to the toilet before breakfast (no doubt was left as to what he did there), and this meant Harriet staying on her own, while her mother was, presumably, still fast asleep. For the first time in our meeting, Mrs H seemed rather embarrassed, not having expected to be shown up like this.

I asked how the parents dealt with Harriet's attempts to use the toilet. She had mentioned how painful defecation was, and I wondered how the parents dealt with this. I was told that Mr H would insist that Harriet should carry on trying, but Mrs H admitted that she could not cope with this and would often interfere and plead on Harriet's behalf, asking her husband to let her go. We tried to imagine how this dialogue unfolded, and we had serious misgivings about the atmosphere that was bound to develop over these situations. But Mrs H volunteered one rationale for her brand of protectiveness of Harriet: "I thought the poor girl must be having the kind of pains one has in childbirth!" We were left to wonder what Harriet made of this supposedly supportive and comforting remark. Considering how recently the baby had been born, labour pains must really have been a topical subject. Mrs H commented that her family doctor was sure that Harriet's problems were linked to the baby's birth, but Mrs H argued that she had complained of the constipation much earlier than the pregnancy and added that Harriet could not possibly know anything of what went on during labour, since she had only heard about pains after the event.

Several times during Mrs H's story, I felt like picking up on some point for more detailed inquiry, but I was worried that, once started, Mrs H would not manage to stop. It was towards the end of the interview that I became certain of what my intuition was warning me against: Mrs H simply loved talking to doctors. As an out-patient, as much as an in-patient, Mrs H was very attached—if not plainly dependent on—a doctor's support. And this attachment could be gratified by consultations about herself as much as when discussing Harriet's problems. It is this assumption that made me understand why Harriet was so afraid of hospitals—I believe she had sensed how important it was for her mother to gain contact with doctors, even if through Harriet's symptoms. On another level, it seemed very likely that Mrs H could not recognize Harriet's own experience of her difficulties.

I tried to discuss the actual events surrounding defecation. Harriet found this somewhat difficult, but Mrs H helped to fill in the picture, and we gradually could recognize that Harriet was able to register her body urges and she knew that she should go to the toilet. She could make her way there, but then she stopped:

something happened at this point when she took her pants down and then found that she could not make herself actually sit on the toilet. I would not expect her to be able to formulate in words what exactly frightened her about that particular step in the sequence, and I asked Harriet if she could perhaps make some drawing.

She drew a Ninja turtle ("like the one I have on my watch", she explained) underground, under the street level, near a manhole (Figure 4.5). The line in the middle of the road showed how the scene was being seen from outside, much as the pavement line clarified this further. The sky was quite empty, but she later coloured it in. She did not pause for long before drawing a second picture (Figure 4.6): this now showed "how it is inside", with water running and dripping all round, all very dark and scary. The size of the manhole gave a likely idea of the intensity of Harriet's anxiety.

This is the point where it is difficult to decide how much to interpret to the child. The fact that she put a creature "inside" would strongly suggest fantasies related to pregnancy, much as the degree of magnification of the manhole might point to further ideas about a baby's growth. I decided to restrict myself to a vaguer statement of her anxiety, and I said that the pictures showed how very different things are when they are seen from outside or when from inside: in the first picture, people would think there is a small hole and they would know nothing of what happens inside, but the second picture showed how things inside are huge, dark, wet and scary. I added that this was probably why she was so afraid of sitting on the toilet, because she did not know what exactly would come out. Harriet nodded her head, confirming that this made sense to her.

Mrs H was fascinated by my comments. She did ask Harriet whether I was right, and Harriet confirmed that I was. We discussed how to proceed, and I went through the ritual of urging Mrs H to institute some sort of fixed time for Harriet to sit on the toilet, but I had little hope that she would manage to do this.

Follow-up appointments were missed, but Mrs H told the clinic's secretary that Harriet was managing to sit on the toilet and defecate normally. According to my paediatric colleagues, Harriet was not brought back again for constipation, but appointments continued to be made for a wide range of other reasons.

Figure 4.5

Figure 4.6

Comment

This was one of many children I have seen who left me with a profound sense of sadness and hopelessness. The development of Harriet's body functions and body image was so intimately linked to her mother's pathology that it would be difficult not to be pessimistic about Harriet's future. When I saw her, reports suggested that she was managing to keep her academic, social, and intellectual development independent from her parents' influence, but for how long would she manage to do this?

Mrs H was offered regular counselling or therapy, which she turned down. We tried to get Harriet into individual psychotherapy, but this never got off the ground. Apparently, the only positive datum that can be reported is Harriet's capacity to convey her unconscious anxieties through her drawings and, luckily, the subsequent suspension of her constipation. But I do not know how her sense of self-control developed later on.

Leon

At the request of the family GP, Leon was seen by a paediatrician when he was 7½ years old. For the previous year, Leon had been messing himself, though he had been in full control of his sphincters before that. The consultant was told that Leon was able to defecate in the toilet once or twice per week, after which his soiling improved for a few days. Physical examination did not reveal any significant abnormality, and the consultant prescribed a small dose of laxatives. He discussed the general situation and urged the parents to make Leon go regularly to the toilet, to help his body to develop a regular rhythm.

When the consultant paediatrician saw Leon one month later, he was told that there had been no change in the situation. He did not feel justified in embarking on complex gastro-intestinal investigations, but at the same time he had been unable to elicit any history of events or experiences that might have represented a traumatic experience for the boy. On balance, he suggested to the parents that, before having further tests, it might be helpful to refer

Leon for a child psychiatric assessment. The parents, Mr and Mrs L, decided that they had nothing to lose by trying out this unexpected recommendation.

Leon and his parents came to see me, and before long we had an atmosphere that could only be described as merry. Leon was a delightful, intelligent boy who was very aware of his problem, and he made it clear that he was eager to find anything that would release him from a symptom that made him feel helpless and ashamed. Mr and Mrs L clearly enjoyed a joke, and they seemed proud of their light-hearted way of facing life and people in general. They accepted my request that they should allow Leon to answer my questions, and they laughed at Leon's answers, though from time to time they would make some funny comment about his stories.

Leon told me about his school life. He was making good progress from an academic point of view, and he had a wide circle of friends, both at school and in his neighbourhood. His mates did not know of the soiling, since this occurred mostly at home; there had been times when he had messed himself when playing with friends outside the house, but he had managed to run home before his friends would know of it. After we talked for some time, I asked Leon to make some drawings while I asked his parents for further information. He was quite willing to do this and soon was concentrating on his drawing, though he followed the conversation closely and put in his own funny comments on what his parents were telling me.

Mr and Mrs L accepted my request to tell me something about their backgrounds; they could understand that knowing about the two of them and also about the development of the family would give me a clearer framework against which to place Leon's difficulties.

Mrs L was the youngest of several children and, from a very young age, was cast in the role of helper and caretaker of her ageing mother. This had led to rather irregular school attendance, and Mrs L had never been able to make up for the learning she had missed out on; she told me, in a self-deprecating tone of voice, that she still struggles with the written word—and, at this point, Mr L interjected that this was one problem they both shared. Whatever I might expect they would feel about such an impediment, I had to accept that, for them, this appeared to be just one more of those facts of life that one has to learn to live with. Mrs L was proud of her marriage, and she claimed to be content with her life, looking after her family and keeping in touch with her extended family.

Mr L also came from a large family. He had grown up among much violence, with frequent rows between the parents and with the children being disciplined through shouts and brute force. He recounted with much laughter that he had wet himself until the age of 7, when one day his father ran after him with a burning piece of paper, threatening to burn him unless he stopped wetting himself. Mr L turned to his wife and, still laughing, asked her "and I never did it again, did I?" She was obviously used to such brand of humour and replied, laughing lovingly, "Never, not once, darling!" Mr L had worked in many different jobs, and for some time now he had been working for a friend of his wife's, an experience that, in spite of his jokes, sounded as if it was quite disastrous.

Predictably, the family had an easy-going style of life, where strictness or discipline were virtually non-existent. At several points, they started discussions to establish how best to answer some question of mine, and soon they would end up laughing, clearly unable to reach any compromise. This occurred, for example, when they wanted to tell me about somebody's age or about the date for some particular event. Mealtimes, ordinary household events—all seemed to take place according to factors that were never predetermined, so that the word "routine" had no application in their daily life. Leaving apart this aspect of family life, there was no doubt that this was a well-integrated, close, warm family.

Leon's soiling had started about eighteen to twenty-four months earlier—the parents were unable to agree on a precise timing. They did, however, manage to agree that the soiling had started not long after Leon had an operation for a squint. He had recovered well from the operation, but he soon developed a pattern of messing, where he would pass a motion about once each week, followed by an improvement in the soiling; but gradually the soiling again increased, irrespective of diets, medication, and many stratagems that the parents had put into practice.

When we were discussing the soiling, it emerged that Leon's younger sibling had also had a brief episode of messing at the time when Leon's encopresis started. Very much in passing, Mr and Mrs L told me that Mrs L's mother had died not much before the children developed these symptoms. We got quite confused when trying to establish the chronological sequence of these events, and at one point the parents were convinced that not much time had passed between these various events I was focusing on, and yet repeatedly they would quote the same "two years ago" or "about one year before" to refer to them. Whatever the real sequence, they insisted that the grandmother's death occurred well before Leon's messing. What surprised me was the unexpected reference to a detail of the circumstances of this grandmother's final illness: she had died after a stroke, but this had first manifested itself by her developing a sudden *squint*. The parents reported the anxiety that had been created in the family by the "slow bleeding in the brain" that had "killed her in one week", but it was obvious that they had never considered that Leon might have made any conscious or unconscious links between his own squint and the significance of the same phenomenon in his grandmother's final illness.

When Leon began to soil himself, Mr L had reacted quite angrily to his messing, and I was told that he had even hit Leon a few times. For her part, Mrs L had resorted to many different ways of dealing with Leon—she had tried to reassure him, just as often as she had criticized him or, at other times, pretended to ignore what was happening. They had consulted the GP and had followed advice given by friends and professionals, but they had never found any measures that produced effective results.

I now turned to Leon's drawings, which he described to us. His first drawing was a rather crude stork (Figure 4.7): he could not explain why he had drawn this, saying only that he knew it was "an African bird". He had next drawn a "Union Jack" (Figure 4.8), but he had "got the colours wrong". The third picture showed a "cowboy" (Figure 4.9), and he told us a long and complicated story about this. His voice became animated while he told us that the cowboy was wearing two trousers and he was shot at by "a little man" (he drew red blobs to mark the places hit by the shots), and four of these had hit "the stomach"; the cowboy had shot himself on the left arm, and Leon said that the little man's eighth shot would kill the cowboy. He now drew a snake (Figure 4.10), using

stake

Figure 4.7

the same black and red pens he had used for the cowboy, but he could not explain why he had drawn each half of the snake with each of these colours.

I thought that Leon's fifth drawing (Figure 4.11) had a different quality compared to the previous ones. He had depicted "a flying fish", but this was surrounded by lines that could both represent waves in the water and also act as disguises to keep the fish hidden from sight. When I asked Leon several questions about this drawing, he seemed rather embarrassed; he laughed, trying to find answers, but these seemed clearly improvised, rather than thoughts that had already been available to him when he originally drew the fish. He told me that he had drawn "a frame" around the fish, and he said that this was "a picture" and not just an illustration of a fish inside a fish-tank.

Leon now picked up another sheet of paper and drew a frame (Figure 4.12), inside which he drew a multitude of lines—he said this was a maze. He could not explain the triangles, but he wrote "in" and "out" to mark the entrance and exit. The parents were making occasional comments about my conversation with Leon, and at this point they mentioned that, for some inexplicable reason, Leon refused to eat solids when he joined the family for an evening meal. I noticed that Leon wrote the "in" sign at the same time that Mr and Mrs L told me of this food habit.

When I thought that it was clear that Leon had finished his drawings, I invited him and his parents to go through all the drawings he had made. I asked what they made of the pictures; Leon did not add anything, and his parents restricted their comments to some adjectives about the quality of the drawings. I of-

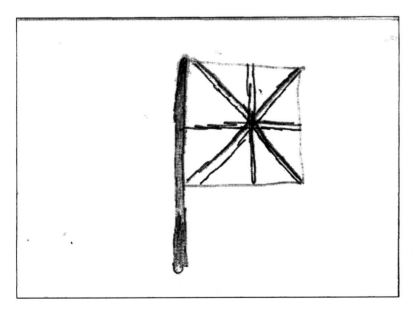

Figure 4.8

Figure 4.9

fered to describe what I thought was a story that was depicted in the pictures. I said nothing about Leon's spelling, but I told him that I suspected that the stork might have something to do with stories about how babies are born. The picture of the flag perhaps indicated his feeling that there was something wrong, not just in the drawing but also somewhere else. The cowboy struck me as bringing into sharp focus a person's belly, with four shots hitting it. The snake appeared to illustrate some division of a unit into two, though I could not say exactly what this referred to. The fish looked to me like Leon's idea of a baby inside his mother's body, and, finally, the maze seemed to depict a very confused idea of the insides of a body, but now no longer a mother's body but any person's—and I suggested that perhaps this was a representation of what Leon thought was the inside of his own body—that is, he can recognize a place for things to go in and another place for them to come out, but he is confused about what goes on inside it, and perhaps the same confusion exists about what might come out of it.

Leon smiled, with a faint touch of recognition of something familiar. Mr and Mrs L laughed, clearly amused at what I was saying, but then Mrs L remembered that two days earlier (no, said her husband, it had been three days earlier) Leon had asked her if it was true that babies were born through the underneath of the body. She answered that yes, that was true. Leon firmly replied that he did not believe her, since one of his friends at school had told him that babies came out of the mothers through their front. Both parents discussed the question of schoolchildren and the problems that result from their exchanging stories, but Leon looked as if he had worked something out. He was looking at me, and I repeated my previous interpretation, but now in different

Figure 4.10

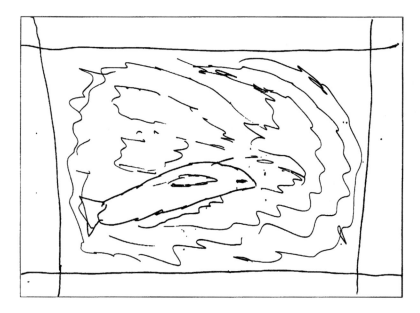

Figure 4.11

words, saying that Leon obviously *knew* some facts about the body, but that he still seemed to *feel* muddled about the possibility that digestion and pregnancy might take place in the same organs.

I now discussed with Mr and Mrs L the importance of helping Leon to develop a routine for his bowels to open every day at the same time; I suggested that they should get him to sit on the toilet each morning and evening, always at the same time. The parents were to make a chart, and Leon would get two points for each day in which he defecated normally, without messing himself. We arranged another appointment for two weeks later, and it was agreed that if Leon reached twenty-eight points, his father would give him an Action Man figure of Leon's choice.

When Leon came back with his parents two weeks later, he was beaming and showing off the Action Man he had been given. Mr and Mrs L showed me the chart, where it was obvious that Leon had scored two points every day of the previous fortnight. The rest of the meeting had the feeling of some celebration. Leon was relieved and proud, apparently confident that he had overcome his problem. Mr and Mrs L were prepared to give some value to their managing to institute some definite routine in their child's life, but they remained incredulous that my interpretation of Leon's anxieties might have played a significant role in the sequence of events. They certainly seemed to believe that Leon had "turned a corner", and it was implied in their comments that they counted on Leon taking responsibility for his bowel movements.

The family contacted me again two weeks later, to say that Leon continued to have effective visits to the toilet every day. We left it that they would get in touch at a later date, if this proved necessary. Some months later I asked the paediatrician and the GP for news on Leon, and as neither had heard from the family again, we had to assume that Leon was doing well.

Figure 4.12

Comment

I would not be able to explain why Leon had started his cycle of constipation and overflow—this seemed to be connected to his grandmother's death and his squint operation, but our interview brought no evidence that this was a relevant datum. Leon's unconscious fantasies over the contents of his body seemed quite central to his anxieties at the time of the interview, but again it would be difficult to prove the presence of these fantasies throughout the months he presented his symptoms. Considering the main points of the consultation, the verbalization of Leon's fantasy seemed to be very important, but we must take into account his parents' initiating and sustaining an attitude of close attention and discipline regarding his going to the toilet. If we are to ask the question as to which of these two played a more significant role in Leon's "cure", I believe we would not have the means of measuring the degree of importance of each of them. However, there were many times when Mr and Mrs L had tried to get Leon to defecate "properly", so this particular occasion when they succeeded in their efforts must be linked to their recognizing that Leon needed strict regularity and persistence on their part and, even more important, finding out how their own childhood experiences had led them to disbelieve that any child in that situation could be actually helped by the adults around him.

The argument could be raised that my recommendation of strict discipline played a major role in bringing the desired improvement, but this advice had already been given to the parents many times before, without any results following from this. I would argue that the relevant factor in our consultation was the combination of Leon understanding the nature of his anxieties and the parents recognizing the need to change their attitude of apparent tolerance and kindness to one of clear support and firmness. The promise of the Action Man reward probably gave Leon a tangible goal to aim for, and I suppose it also allowed Mr and Mrs L to recognize that they had an active part in the search for success. In other words, instead of being caught up in a vicious circle of despondency and helplessness, they could all try to engage in a mutually reinforcing circle of encouragement and success.

A final point arises from the information that only a few days before the interview, Leon had asked his mother questions about childbirth. I have seen another child, "Penny" (Brafman, 1997, p. 781), who made a picture of a bee, and this turned out to be one of the key points to understand her conflicts. We then learnt that she had been involved with a bee only days before the interview. Would this chronological sequence then signify that the consultation elicited and recognized an unconscious fantasy that had only appeared days before the interview—and would this, therefore, raise doubts about the validity of hypothesizing that this fantasy underlay the symptoms over the months preceding these recent events? This point can be argued both ways, since it is possible to imagine that Penny's and Leon's interest in these matters was brought to the fore because they knew they were due to see someone who might be able to help them with their difficulties. If this was the case, then this would constitute further evidence to substantiate Winnicott's argument that the child seemed to have started a relationship with him *before* actually coming to see him. I certainly find this hypothesis very plausible.

CHAPTER FIVE

Virtually only the child

In the next three cases, the consultation unfolds almost irrespectively of the parents' contribution. Two children presenting with nightmares were freed of them, without the parents quite grasping why this should be so; the third child had a distant, but perhaps supportive mother, who was not present at the consultation.

"Mary" was clearly determined to get some help from me, and she pursued this even if her mother was baffled—if not displeased—with the course of the consultation. Like Leon (chapter four), Mary got engrossed in her pictures, and she simply produced a whole series of these, giving the impression of putting her dreams on paper. When once presenting this case, I was praised for my "intuition", but however plausible this idea can be, I remain convinced that I can "guess" the meaning of the drawings because I look at them, from the beginning, as the representation of an image that the child wants to convey to me. In Mary's pictures, I knew she had nightmares, and from the moment she named her picture "mummy" and explained her efforts to "make her look pretty", I was looking out for further cues related to the mother's state or condition. The mother was one of the most sceptical parents I have met, and seldom have I seen someone who has left a consultation feeling so upset and resentful.

"Trevor's" father seemed to have no conception of a child having a mind of his own. Not having met his mother, I cannot comment on her view of Trevor. The boy was definitely not psychologically minded, and he tackled the consultation much as he probably dealt with anything else in his life—copying his father, it was all a big laugh, as long as people were friendly and respectful. All through our meeting, I was aware that I could not afford to displease Mr T and that, as long as he was joking and answering my questions, Trevor could continue to talk and, eventually, produce his picture. Considering the disappearance of Trevor's nightmares and sleepwalking after this consultation, I could only surmise that my interpretation of his picture brought to his consciousness the nature of his fears.

"Paula's" consultation and her drawings are the most gratifying in my clinical experience. Not only did she show remarkable changes and improvement, but her superimposed pictures are perhaps the most dramatic in my collection, and her squiggle sequence is also exceptional in its dénouement. But the mother was not present in the consulting-room (I saw Paula many years ago), and her role in Paula's progress is a good subject for discussion. Overtly, she was hostile to my work, but I believe that her support was an invaluable factor in Paula's progress.

Mary

The GP referred Mary, aged 4 years, for a psychiatric assessment because

"in the last three weeks she wakes up in the night, screaming and then goes into a trance-like state; her teachers say she is disruptive and naughty at school. Her mother has been advised by the school to seek professional help. Mary has had sodium cromoglycate and more recently terbutaline sulphate for chronic coughs and coughing on exercise which I thought was asthma. We think she had chickenpox one month ago."

The phrasing of the letter clearly indicated that the doctor was agreeing to the formality of a medical referral, whilst reserving his views about the need for such a consultation: the school requested/recommended help; Mary's mother, Mrs M, was prepared to accept this; and the doctor complied. While noting the possible implications of this apparent dynamic configuration, an appointment was sent for Mary and her parents to come to the clinic.

In fact, only Mary and her mother attended for the appointment. After I had gone through my usual steps of greeting them and trying to make them feel comfortable, Mary moved towards the table with toys and Mrs M told me that, from her point of view, her daughter had two different problems: one, her disturbed sleep, and two, her "impossible behaviour" at home and at school.

Mrs M was in her 30s, though she looked much younger. She had stopped working when Mary was born, and she now had a second child. Mr M was described as a quiet man who avoided confrontations at all costs. Mrs M saw this as a problem when he tried to pacify Mary rather than disciplining her firmly, as Mrs M would like him to do. The couple had met when both of them were working abroad, and they had lived in other countries for several years before returning home to England.

Mrs M told me that Mary had always been difficult: she "will never do as she is told", "she is disobedient, defiant, always running around". When Mary went to a local nursery, Mrs M felt that "the teachers didn't like her", to judge from comments they made. Mrs M had visited the nursery and thought that the children were left to their own devices, never properly helped to concentrate on constructive activities. She moved Mary to another nursery, but again she was told that Mary is never still, does not obey the teachers, and so on. As regards life at home, Mary "turns every minor daily chore into a big issue", and Mrs M quoted Mary refusing to put her shoes on. If Mr M is home and gets involved, Mrs M complained that he "just takes her off to do something different", which Mrs M considers a sign of disrespect for her authority, besides allowing Mary to ignore her responsibilities as a growing child. There was no doubt that Mrs M felt intensely challenged and disrespected by Mary and by her husband.

Considering the moves that the family had made before and after Mary's birth and also the recent arrival of a younger sibling, I tried to explore whether Mrs M thought that these factors might have influenced the structuring of the couple's life, as well as Mary's development. Mrs M did not agree with me. She was trying hard to hide her impatience with questions I asked about herself and her husband. There was no avoiding the fact that Mrs M thought there was "something wrong" in Mary and that this is what she wanted me to take as my starting point, if not as the only focus of my attention.

Mary had been playing with various toys on a table in a quiet and competent manner, and I called Mrs M's attention to this, asking her if this was in any way significant; she became quite upset and asked me if I was telling her that she was wasting my time. I explained that what had occurred to me was the possibility that, when interested in something, Mary was able to concentrate and play in a constructive way—in other words, perhaps the nursery was not giving her adequate stimulation? Mrs M dismissed this, out of hand, reminding me of what happened all the time at home. I thought that Mrs M's anxiety about Mary seemed out of proportion to the examples she was giving me, but I found no way of reassuring her or of obtaining any clues to what might be causing such intense worry in her. I was struck by the fact that Mary responding so well to her father's approach was taken as a provocation rather than a reassurance, but again I found no room to explore this further.

Mrs M told me about the night-time crises: Mary starts to scream and one or both parents try to wake her up, but even when she stops screaming, Mary will go into a kind of trance which the parents cannot affect, until eventually she returns to sleep. Mrs M had no idea how best to deal with these episodes. If I might be interested in what caused these episodes, Mrs M wanted to know how to eliminate them. I am sure she was concerned by Mary's distress, but she sounded as if it was the disturbance of the family's sleep that she objected to.

During this conversation, Mary had been playing with the dolls' house. She had arranged some pieces of furniture to make up a kitchen and breakfast-room. A daddy and a mummy were preparing breakfast for the baby and a little girl, who were playing together. She managed to stand the wire dolls neatly against the kitchen counter, and she was muttering words to indicate a friendly conversation between the parents, occasionally moving over to the children and then making them play in a similar friendly fashion. I was struck by the dexterity with which she moved the toys and the quiet tone of the events unfolding in the game. After a while, Mary decided to play with something else, and she explored the materials on the table. I offered her some jigsaw puzzles, but she dismissed them. She did not seem to like the other toys, and I asked her if she would perhaps like to draw: her face lit up with a wonderful smile. I gave her some sheets of paper and a pack of felt-tip pens, and she promptly chose one. She held it firmly and proceeded to draw a circle and various lines inside and outside it (Figure 5.1). Most of the dots in this picture, however, were actually added later, towards the end of the interview.

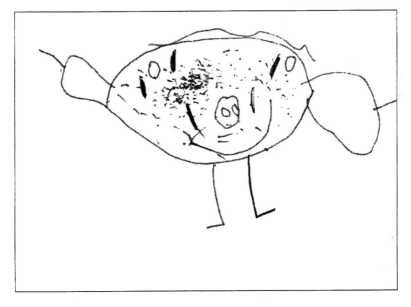

Figure 5.1

I could recognize the shapes for mouth, eyes, nose, and legs, but I decided to check on those coming out of the side of the face. "Arms!", Mary said, almost angrily, as if I had doubted whether she knew what she had drawn. I asked if the picture showed someone in particular, and she said "Mummy". What about the spots on the face? "To make her look nice." She now pushed the paper aside and made another drawing: a spider (Figure 5.2). This one took less time to make, and she promptly moved on to the next sheet, a frog with a tail and a turtle fish (Figure 5.3). Mary could not or did not want to give any explanations about her chosen subjects, though her choice of colours and the determination with which she drew her shapes would point to her having a firm idea about what was on her mind. Her next two pictures depicted money (Figure 5.4) and buttons (Figure 5.5).

The next drawing (Figure 5.6) was quite elaborate: she first made yellow circles with tail-like lines coming out of them, then a long row of red circles running in parallel to the yellow circles. She put some red and blue lines inside the yellow shapes and then

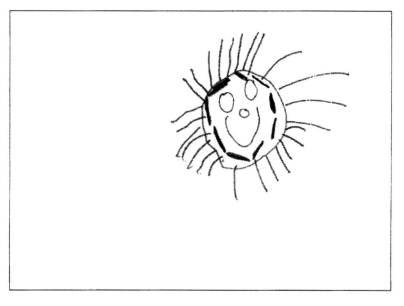

Figure 5.2

Figure 5.3

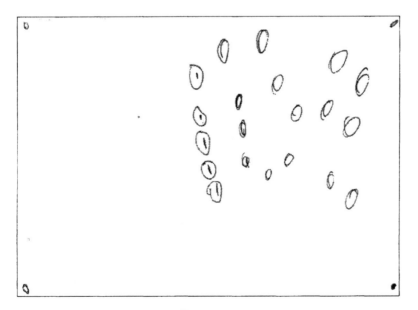

Figure 5.4

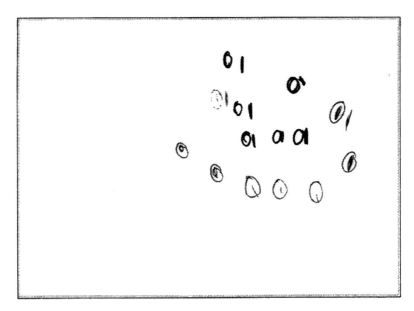

Figure 5.5

Figure 5.6

130

more yellow circles with lines at the top of the page, followed by red ones underneath. Finally, she added scribbles on the top left of the picture, drawn with quite a different movement of the hand. I asked Mary to tell me about the picture, and she told me about the various elements but slowly moved away from the table and sat down on a nearby settee, still explaining the drawing, but now also showing me her foot at the same time. The yellow circles were "rocks"; these were stones where crabs could hide underneath, but then they would come out and "pinch your foot", which was very painful. After a pause, I asked about the scribbles on the top left of the page, and Mary explained that this was her name.

Mary went back to the table and drew with relish, perhaps even excitement. She made a crab with many crab/circles inside (Figure 5.7). She explained that the little crabs grow bigger and bigger. She then drew the circles outside the original one. Finally, she added some shapes which she called "letters". As she finished these, she put the pen down and sat back on the chair, making it quite clear that she had no wish to make any further drawings.

Figure 5.7

Mrs M had followed this sequence with interest, though her face showed her bafflement, perhaps wondering what would come out of all this. I asked her what she had made of the drawings, and she made a dismissive face, adding "Nothing, really". I explained to Mrs M that I wanted to ask Mary some questions, but that I was keen not to put words in her mouth. I went through each drawing with Mary, to make sure that I had understood her descriptions. I then commented on the fact that the shapes she had used for money, buttons, and crabs were all similar circles, and Mary nodded her head, as if this should have been obvious. I asked her whether there was any connection between these circles and the dots she had put on the first picture. She nodded vigorously, saying an emphatic "Yes!" and, picking up the green pen, proceeded to put more and more dots on "mother's" face. Mrs M now looked bewildered, almost irritated, as if I were encouraging Mary to continue her drawing nonsense. I tried to engage Mrs M's interest in the content of the pictures, but she definitely failed to see any significance in them.

I now had a difficult problem. However much Mrs M could recognize that Mary was engaged in some meaningful communication with me, I felt quite convinced that she was not pleased with my apparently ignoring the problems that she considered important. By now, I was sure that Mrs M was bound to dismiss any advice I might come to give her regarding Mary's problems. I thought that she had sensed, quite correctly, that I saw Mary's behaviour problems as secondary to her emotional conflicts and that it was these emotional elements that had monopolized my attention. Mrs M wanted a clear medical diagnosis of Mary's condition and a prescription that would not involve anyone other than Mary herself. But, however aware I was of these feelings of Mrs M, I felt unable to forget the fact that Mary had done her best to convey her feelings to me, and I did not want to let her down. I was quite worried that Mrs M might object to what I wanted to say, but I decided to take the risk, in the hope that this might help Mary to deal with her anxieties.

I said to Mary that I thought her drawings showed what happened in her dreams: at the beginning, her mother had "a nice face", but then spots appeared on it that gradually turned into dangerous, attacking, hurtful crabs—and I added that Mary might be afraid that it was she herself who was hurting and upsetting her mother. It was at this point of my explanation that Mary went back to her first drawing and proceeded to insert a multitude of further dots on the "mother's face". If we wanted to pick out an element of hostility in Mary's feelings towards her mother, these "further injuries" would represent the best evidence—if she was afraid of hurting her mother, here would be the corresponding unconscious wish to inflict such hurt. If I had been seeing Mary alone, I might have voiced this interpretation, but I would not make this explicit when her mother was sitting next to us. I mentioned the suspected "chickenpox" that Mary had suffered some weeks earlier as the source of the "dots on the face" as signs of some damage.

Mrs M now voiced her disbelief with barely contained anger. What I had said was absurd, too far-fetched to be true. I suggested that she might ask Mary what she thought, and, as Mrs M did this, Mary nodded vigorously, saying that yes, this was how her dreams were. Mrs M appeared to believe Mary's words, and I was relieved at that demonstration of trust and acceptance. I tried to explain to Mrs M that children tend to create their own interpretations of their daily experiences, but some of these constructions are relegated to the child's unconscious, so that when they turn up in dreams children can be very frightened, as if their worst fears were turning into reality. There was a possibility that Mary's facial lesions of the recent possible chickenpox had led her to consider them as a sign of badness or danger. Mrs M tried hard to show a polite attitude to these explanations, which were clearly not very convincing to her, but Mary was now quite relaxed and peaceful, again playing with the dolls' house, as if giving us time to round off the interview.

I asked Mrs M whether she wanted to ask me any questions, as she seemed to want something quite different from our meeting, but she could not find anything to say. I thought that she might want to see me without Mary being present, and I offered to see her again on her own or with her husband. Besides trying to offer Mrs M an opportunity to discuss how best to approach the issue of disciplining Mary, I was also interested to discover the source for Mrs M's conviction that Mary harboured some serious pathology. In the event, Mrs M just said that she "would think about it and speak to her husband" and let me know of their decision.

One week later, Mrs M telephoned the clinic and said that, since the day of the consultation, Mary had not had any further nightmares and was now sleeping through the night. Regarding further appointments, she said that these were not necessary for the time being. I telephoned the GP some weeks later, and he told me that Mrs M had been to see him for some problem with the baby and she then told him that Mary was sleeping normally. I did not obtain any follow-up regarding Mary's behaviour at school.

Discussion

Mary's case is precious evidence for my belief that the help a child gets is entirely dependent on the particular professional who sees her. Though Mary's nightmares caused considerable distress to her parents, her mother was mostly worried about her behaviour, and this had been the element that determined the school's advice for help to be sought. Had Mrs M been referred to a psychologist who focused on behaviour modification, this would have been the treatment Mary would have received. A paediatrician might have prescribed some tranquillizing medication, much as another psychologist could have opted for some counselling for Mrs M, and an educational psychologist might have decided to work with Mary's teachers during visits to the school. Mrs M's account of her clashes with her husband were sufficient indication for some marital counselling. At the end of the day, Mrs M wanted something done *with* and *for* Mary. It is quite conceivable that, whatever benefit followed from my intervention, Mrs M still sought further consultations with other professionals regarding Mary's problems.

There is no doubt that had Mary been referred to a colleague, the interview was bound to have followed quite a different course, but the moment I offered Mary to draw I had no option but to take into account her response: from the first few lines, Mary seemed quite determined to convey some message to me. There is no question of her being consciously aware of *expressing* something in her drawings, but she must have been continuously monitoring my response to each successive drawing. I can only conclude that she felt that I was "passing the test", because she continued to draw and tell me the stories for each picture until she came to the letters in the last picture, when she put the pens down in the manner of someone who has finished what they wanted to say.

Mrs M's reaction when I gave my interpretation of the drawings poses quite an interesting problem. Intellectually, she found my ideas absurd, but she was able to respect Mary's reaction to them. Should one ignore this? Or should one praise her for believing in her child? The danger here is the consultant being seen as taking sides with the child against the mother, which makes me tend not to comment on this change of views on the parent's part. I would, however, assume that if Mrs M could accept that Mary was not setting out to defy her but, rather, expressing conflicts that she could not cope with, then this may well have led her to offer Mary a different emotional atmosphere when putting her to bed.

For her part, Mary is not the first child I have met whose symptoms disappear as soon as they find someone putting their unconscious anxieties into words.

From a psychoanalytic perspective, Mary's probably aggressive impulses towards her mother could be recognized in the manner in which she returned to her first drawing to "inflict" further dots/ crabs on her; similarly, the second picture (Figure 5.2) indicates fantasies related to pregnancy and quite probably to hostile impulses related to the birth of Mary's younger sibling. If Mary did go into individual therapy, these fantasies would be explored at length, but in the context of this first (and, as I feared, only) meeting, I chose not to mention these possible conflicts.

The findings in this interview would lead me to think that Mary's "impossible behaviour" was strongly linked to the reported conflicts between her parents regarding her disciplining. Ideally, I would recommend that Mr and Mrs M should be seen together to explore the reasons for such disagreements. If these marital meetings could lead the parents to deal with Mary in a more coherent manner, it is quite probable that this would produce an improvement in Mary's behaviour. If this approach was not acceptable to the parents, then some individual work with Mary would certainly be advisable.

This case is presented here as an example of diagnostic interviews where it is clear that the child behaves as if expecting to obtain help from the consultant. Assuming that the follow-up we obtained is reliable, then Mary did manage to escape from her nightmares—many colleagues will argue that if this symptom has disappeared, the underlying conflicts have still remained, and I would entirely agree with this view. However, rightly or wrongly, I felt that I had to respond to Mary there and then. The alternative would have been to leave aside Mary's pictures and her stories and to have focused on Mrs M's questions. But I was convinced that I would never manage to reassure her regarding Mary's mental health, nor was Mrs M allowing me to obtain sufficient evidence to recognize what exactly made her so worried about Mary. I could only hope that Mrs M might agree to give me another opportunity to investigate other aspects of Mary's and the family's life, but for that moment in time I decided not to ignore Mary's plea for help.

Trevor

Trevor was referred by his GP because he had had disturbed nights for the last six months. He had night terrors, sleepwalking episodes, or nightmares most nights, and the parents felt desperate for some help. The doctor mentioned that one of Trevor's siblings was being assessed by the school educational psychologist because of behaviour problems and general lack of academic progress. She also warned me that Trevor's "parents, particularly his father, are of rather tempestuous temperaments". I had, indeed, heard stories from my psychologist colleague at the clinic that more than justified the doctor's warning. The parents, Mr and Mrs T, were passionately opposed to professionals and to authority figures in general, and the teachers at their children's schools knew how careful they had to be with their words when they had to address these parents.

Mr T brought Trevor to see me. Trevor was quite short, but his posture and demeanour suggested a mature boy, older than his 9 years of age. Trevor spoke easily and fast, his words sharp, almost cutting. He was polite, respectful, certainly not afraid of meeting a psychiatrist. Whatever his parents thought of doctors in general and psychiatrists in particular, Trevor seemed oblivious to any idea that there was anything different or special about me to differentiate me from any other adult. He answered my questions about school life, telling me that he was a popular boy, with many friends who liked him and enjoyed playing together. No, he did not have "a best friend", but this was not seen as important by him. Trevor seemed quite happy with school life, though I was not convinced that he saw school as a place where he would have anything to learn. Teachers were described rather in terms of their nuisance value, and Trevor could not name any subject he particularly favoured. Life in the neighbourhood where they lived was described as wonderful, with many mates with whom to share various adventures. He liked his older brother, in spite of their frequent confrontations, and he did not mind the idiosyncrasies of his younger siblings. Trevor also mentioned his wider family: both parents had grown up locally, and they had a very close family, with many uncles, aunts, and cousins.

Mr T was of average height and quite muscular. He wore sporty clothes, and his short, cropped hair created a prickly appearance that was only accentuated by his curt and punchy way of speaking. Mr T obviously wanted to look young and trendy, a young man of the world, not a "paterfamilias". He told me quite openly of his displeasure at the idea of his son seeing a psychiatrist, but he trusted the family doctor ("she has been the family doctor for yonks and we all like her") and this had been her recommendation, so he was complying. Furthermore, he was concerned about his son's problems and if I could help him to overcome them, then he did not mind coming to see me. Mr T told me how Trevor had been waking up most nights in a terrible panic. Trevor would run around the rooms of the house, crying and flailing his arms, with one or both parents behind him, trying to hold him and to give him some comfort while he pushed them away, as if they represented further threats to him. Clearly, the point had been reached where the whole family dreaded the nights, always expecting that Trevor might wake up again.

Mr T told me of one occasion when he tried to reassure Trevor by telling him that there was no need for him to be so afraid, since both his parents loved him. Considering the flow of our conversation up that point, this language seemed quite different from what I had heard, so I was not surprised to hear that Mr T was quite taken aback by Trevor's reply: the boy had asked him whether his brothers and sisters also loved him. Mr T handled this in a most inspired way. He not only confirmed that Trevor's siblings loved him, but he also wrote down on a piece of paper that each of them loved Trevor and suggested that he should keep this piece of paper under his pillow. Trevor did do exactly that, making sure that nobody touched it, holding on to that scrap of paper as if it were a talisman.

Mr T worked as a roofer. His work kept him away from home for long hours, but he felt that he had an active role in the family's life. He spent many hours at weekends playing with the children, but he believed that the everyday details of the children's lives belonged to his wife's area of responsibility. School, meals, life in the neighbourhood, behaviour towards each other and to adults, and so forth were left to Mrs T—and, even though he was quite forceful in these assertions, I could not avoid a suspicion that husband and wife had developed a pattern of relationship where such a division was more apparent than real. According to him, Mr T was "summoned" or called into action when there was a crisis, but it was obvious that they worked in unison and that the children had learnt to treat injunctions as originating from both parents, irrespective of which one conveyed these to them.

I thought that it would be difficult to discover details of life at home, and I was not sure, at that point, of how relevant these would be in trying to help Trevor over his night terrors. I decided to follow the cues that Trevor and his father gave me, without asking questions that they might interpret as probing into areas they wanted to preserve from me. First, this would prevent any unnecessary antagonism, but, second, I also believed that they would unconsciously lead me to the relevant conflicts.

As they seemed to make themselves comfortable, Mr T warmed up and told me with pride of Trevor's attitude to the world. Trevor was, visibly, a true miniature replica of his father, not only physically but also in his language and attitudes. I commented on Trevor's sense of humour and his occasional grimacing, and Mr T told me that all the family knew of Trevor's "clowning". This led

Mr T to tell me of his spending his own time with his mates in a pub, where they relaxed from their taxing work by compulsive joking and mutual teasing. Very much following the flow of this account, Mr T went on to mention how he would often take Trevor with him to work when the boy did not have to attend school. Trevor had become something of a pet to the whole team of roofers with whom Mr T worked. He would sometimes join in their chattering and bantering, and the group often gave Trevor tasks related to their work.

Mr T told me of an occasion when he was on top of a high roof, having told Trevor to wait for him on the ground. Suddenly, he discovered that Trevor's head was popping up over the roof edge, a happy, triumphant grin on his mischievous face; somehow, Mr T managed to smile, and he beckoned Trevor to join him, uttering words of pride and encouragement. As soon as Trevor got near him, Mr T grabbed him and sighed with relief that the boy was now safe. Significantly, he made little mention to me about reprimanding the boy. I thought the emphasis here was on the extent to which Trevor took after him, and the father's pride seemed by far to overshadow his awareness that Trevor had exposed himself to dangers that he could not appreciate.

During most of this conversation, Trevor had been making a drawing. He was sitting near me, keeping the sheet of paper on my desk, while Mr T sat at some distance, by a window. The atmosphere in the room was quite relaxed, and by now Mr T was clearly seeing me as someone who could appreciate his feelings of concern and pride for his son. I voiced my admiration for his sensitivity and sangfroid, adding in a joking tone of voice that I had always thought of roofers as tough, dour people—he replied that he knew this was exactly how everybody thought of his profession ("tough and nasty", he said), but that "when it comes to children I go really soft".

I thought that Trevor had finished his drawing, and he confirmed my impression. I suggested that we should invite his father to come closer and join us at the desk. I explained to Mr T that children sometimes used drawings to express things that they were unable to put into words. Particularly when it came to dreams, and even more so with nightmares, children tended to be inhibited about turning them into stories, but that quite often they would convey in pictures some of the thoughts or feelings that worried or frightened them.

Trevor had drawn a house with several clouds floating around in the air (Figure 5.8). I asked him to describe his picture, and he went through the colours and distribution of door and windows. I asked if this was a house he knew—no. Had he ever seen it?—no. Did anyone live there?—no. I asked if there was a story attached to the drawing, and he confirmed my impression that he had not built any story around it. Mr T looked on, interested but puzzled. Having explored whatever Trevor might have consciously attached to the house, I called his attention to the roof. He was puzzled, and he looked at me as if wondering what I would ask next. I just kept looking at him and at the roof, and it was Mr T who came into the conversation and pointed out how sloped it was. Trevor burst out in a huge smile, acknowledging how dangerous it would be for anyone to work on that roof.

Figure 5.8

I thought that after all the tales of courage, daring, and bravado, we now had evidence of how aware Trevor was of the danger surrounding his father's work. I asked him if he had been following our conversation, and he confirmed that he had done so and had heard his father's account of the day when he had himself climbed onto a high roof. I asked Trevor if the house he had drawn might perhaps be anything like what he saw in his nightmares, and, much to his father's surprise, he nodded, with a totally different kind of smile on his face: now he showed relief. I did put into words that anyone having to work on that roof was in serious danger of falling and getting hurt—and that I thought that it did worry him to know this was the situation to which his father was exposed as part of his daily work. Mr T was very surprised at my words and asked Trevor whether this was correct. Fortunately, Trevor mumbled, "Yes, it's true . . .".

We made an appointment for three weeks' time to check on progress. Trevor and his father came to see me, with the same air of camaraderie and light-heartedness they had shown when we first met. They were pleased with how life had gone on—Trevor had slept through all nights, and there was no question of distressing dreams. Mr T recounted the conversation he had had with his wife about the boy's drawing and my comments. Mrs T was not surprised, and she told Mr T that his perception of his job was definitely not what she or any outsider thought of it. But there was no question of his giving up his work, since he clearly found in it most of what life meant for him. They left me with the impression that nothing would really change in the family's pattern of relationships—except for the fact that Trevor might now have quieter nights.

Paula

Paula, aged 13 years, had been attending a School for Delicate Children (these were schools for children with medical conditions, but they were also used to provide education for children with emotional and/or behaviour difficulties who could not cope with the demands of ordinary school classes). Her teachers felt that her earlier physical problems no longer justified keeping her out of ordinary school, and she was transferred to the local secondary school. Paula found this transition very difficult and began to show signs of distress, which became increasingly severe, and eventually she refused to attend school. Paula's mother, Mrs P, spoke to the teachers. They were agreeable that Paula should be allowed to return to her former school, but the educational authorities demanded a child psychiatric assessment before reversing their decision, and she was referred to our child guidance clinic.

Paula, who started to walk at 18 months and only began to speak when she was 4 years old, had a long medical history. She suffered frequent attacks of bronchitis and pneumonia up to the age of 9 months. At that age, a doctor prescribed some codeine mixture, and it turned out that Paula was allergic to this: she went into coma and was admitted to hospital. She was blind for three days, but she improved and was discharged after one week. During a preliminary meeting with the clinic's social worker, Mrs P told her how she went into the hospital to feed Paula but "she rejected me, even though she took the food from the nurses". When she was about 3 years old, a heart murmur was discovered. Paula was then under observation for several years, though when I saw her she had no heart problems. Paula had also presented a squint, for which she was treated, and her mother told us that Paula had been left with "practically no vision in one eye". Another problem area was Paula's weight; she was described as "eating for comfort", and Mrs P told us that after her husband's death, two years previously, Paula had "started to put on 3 lb each day, without eating much".

Paula apparently had no difficulties attending primary school, although she did have considerable learning problems and required special help; this "didn't help much", and Paula was kept in primary school for an extra year. That autumn her father died, and "Paula went into a state of shock for some time". Paula was now meant to start secondary school, but after lengthy discussions she was given a place at the School for Delicate Children, and Mrs P felt that "Paula simply blossomed there", taking part in all activities and improving her work. To all this complex history of medical and educational problems was added the information that Paula had suffered from enuresis all her life, "except for the period when she attended the special school". However, since she had been transferred to the ordinary secondary school, the wetting had reappeared.

Mrs P described Paula as sensitive, frail, weak, sickly, dependent, miserable, and lacking in confidence—conversely, in their report, the school spoke of Paula as a tall, healthy girl, who preferred the company of boys and enjoyed playing football and cricket.

When asked about Paula's father, Mrs P said that Mr P had suffered from a gastric ulcer for many years. At one point, his doctors decided he would benefit from surgery, and he was admitted to the local general hospital. Unfortunately, one week after returning home from his operation, he had a massive haemorrhage: Paula found him covered in blood, sitting on the toilet. She had screamed for her mother. When Mrs P came to the bathroom, they thought he was dead, but then they noticed some movement and rushed to call an ambulance, which took Mr P to hospital. Mrs P travelled with him in the ambulance, and she told us that she had suggested that Paula should join them, but Paula had refused this, saying that she preferred to go to her school. In hospital, Mr P underwent emergency surgery but died a few days later.

Mrs P was a tense, short woman with a round face and staring, unblinking eyes. She had another child, who was described as "clever, but a poor mixer since childhood". Mrs P said that they had virtually no contact with relatives, since she felt that they were too antagonistic to herself and her children.

Paula was dressed in such a way that when the social worker and I went to the waiting-room to meet them, we thought she was a boy. We all went to the social worker's room, where introductions were made, and we tried to make Paula and her mother feel welcome. Mrs P soon made it clear that she had only agreed to attend because she saw this interview as the price to pay in order to obtain Paula's transfer to her former school. She didn't "believe in discussing the future, since you cannot prevent or change what happens", and as for the past, "it is best to forget or ignore problems because nothing is gained from thinking about them". For her part, Paula was monosyllabic and uncooperative; when asked about her reasons for not attending her present school, she could only say "it is too big". After a while, I thought Paula might be more responsive if I saw her on her own, and we moved to another room, leaving Mrs P with the social worker.

Paula now appeared, indeed, more relaxed, though she did not seem to find it so easy to articulate her thoughts. I apologized for the hesitation in addressing her in the waiting-room and explained that our first impression was of her being a young boy. She nodded and said that for some time now she had thought of herself as a boy. I acknowledged this, but I made no comment at this point. Taking it for granted that the episode of her father's haemorrhage would have been a major trauma for her, I asked Paula about this. She told me about finding her father on the toilet, after her mother told her to call him. She had screamed, and when Mrs P came upstairs she thought he was dead but then noticed some movement and they called the ambulance. Paula confirmed her mother's account that she had asked Paula if she wanted to accompany them, but Paula said she preferred to go to school: she could not give me an explanation for this choice. She shrugged her shoulders and made a rather painful grimace, but she could not muster any words to justify her decision. When I asked her about subsequent events, she told me that she had never cried when she learnt that her father had died. We went on to talk about her "feeling [she] was a boy"; this change had started two years later, but again she could give no explanations. I asked Paula whether she thought there was any link between this change and her father's death, but she denied any such connection.

I noticed that Paula was looking at some paper on my desk, and I suggested that she made a drawing. After some hesitation, she drew a house (Figure 5.9). I did not make any comment, and, after a brief pause, she added a tree, with apples falling from it. I found this a rather unusual picture and asked her about the manner in which she had drawn the apples, but Paula could not clarify this, merely shrugging her shoulders and barely muttering "I don't know". After a brief pause, she went on to draw in a slide, a swing, a see-saw, and benches. Much as with the house, I was struck by the barrenness of the picture, and I called her attention to it: she could not comment on this. Considering that she had drawn these various playground elements, I asked her whether she also drew people. She answered that she only did so with "match-stick" images, and she proceeded to draw a girl skipping rope and some

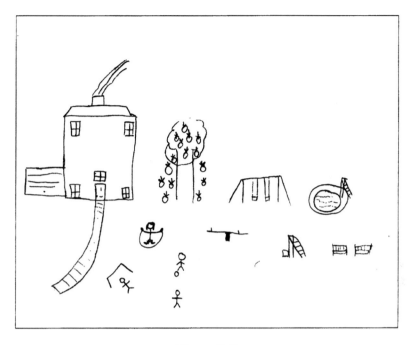

Figure 5.9

boys playing football. "I used to like to be like the girl, but now I prefer to play with the boys", she said.

Here was a spontaneous reference to the question of her gender identity, and I was obviously interested in this. But, taking into account her difficulties with words, I suggested that she might draw these various images of herself. She picked up another page and drew herself "as [she] used to be" (Figure 5.10, top left). Because "this went wrong", she crossed out this drawing and started another one (top middle: long hair and skirt); then drew "how [she] became" (top right: long hair and trousers); and finally, "what [she is] like now" (bottom left: short hair and trousers). Having finished these drawings, Paula waited for my comments. I did think the pictures depicted quite clearly the features that would identify her as "girlish" or, conversely, "boyish", but besides acknowledging this fact, I hesitated, not quite certain as to how to proceed. But Paula had left the two sheets of paper (Figures 5.9 and 5.10) together, and, in line with my previous experience with interviews

Figure 5.10

Figure 5.11

where children made two sequential drawings, I put the two pictures on top of each other, as if they corresponded to a single mental picture that had been split over two different pages. I lifted the two superimposed pages and held them against the light coming from the window (Figure 5.11). When Paula saw the falling apples and the girl's face matching each other so perfectly, she said "she is crying".

I had no doubt in my mind that the tears were a reference to her "never crying" when she found her father and, later, when he died. But I could not just throw this assumption on Paula, as if coming only from my preconceptions. The drawings she had made, up to that point, did not seem to contain any pointers to the *cause* of the tears, and I thought it would be much more useful if we could obtain further clues that might help Paula herself to understand where the tears on the girl's face were coming from. However, because it was so difficult to engage Paula in a dialogue, I suggested we play squiggles. She accepted this and was quickly immersed in the game, one of us drawing a squiggle, then the other completing it.

1. Paula turned my first squiggle into "an animal" (Figure 5.12).
2. I turned her squiggle into a fly (Figure 5.13).
3. She made a bee out of my line (Figure 5.14).
4. I used her line to make a woman holding something on her lap (Figure 5.15).
5. She made a "smiling male frog": because of the way we were sitting at the table, this appeared to be looking at me and I voiced this comment, but she did not so much as smile (Figure 5.16).
6. I hesitated over her squiggle, and she said she knew what it was. I suggested that she should finish it, and she turned it into a monster. I asked about the line on the body, and she said this was a pocket (Figure 5.17).
7. She drew a final squiggle for me to complete (Figure 5.18a).
8. I turned her squiggle into a man sitting on a toilet (Figure 5.18b). I was quite convinced that my picture was no more than the obvious conclusion of the drawing she had started.

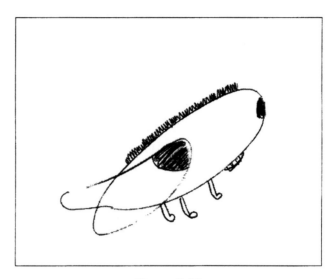

Figure 5.12

Figure 5.13

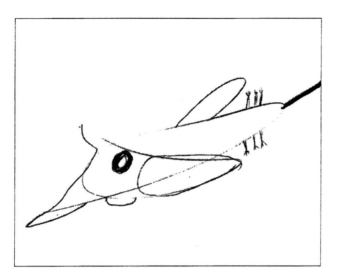

Figure 5.14

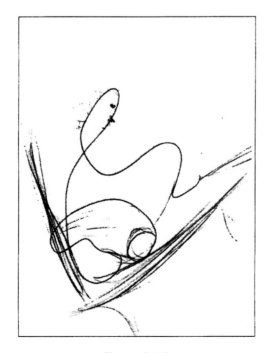

Figure 5.15

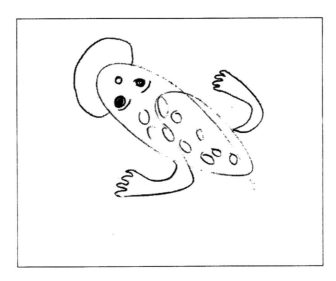

Figure 5.16

Figure 5.17

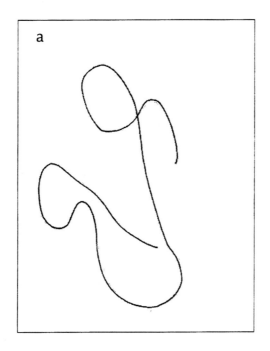

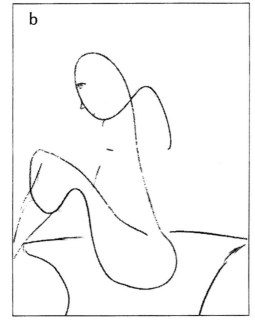

Figure 5.18

Paula showed no surprise at my drawing (Figure 5.18b) or at my putting into words that her squiggle gave the essential lines of the picture of her father as she had found him two years earlier. I suggested that his death and the manner in which it had happened had affected Paula very deeply. I said that she needed help to work out her feelings about it and that I should see her a few more times—but it was impossible for me to discern how my words were affecting Paula. Her face only showed an expression suggestive of acceptance, but she uttered no words. I asked Paula if there were any questions she might want to ask me, but she just shook her head, making a grimace as if to indicate that she had nothing to say. After a pause, I suggested that we should rejoin her mother and the social worker.

I told Mrs P that I would be happy to recommend Paula's return to her former school, but I added that I believed that Paula should have some further individual interviews, since I did not think that the school transfer alone would be enough to help her with her problems. Mrs P made it clear that she disagreed with me. She repeated her earlier statement that she was quite convinced that returning to her old school was all that Paula needed to make her again the happy and successful girl she had been. There was absolutely no justification for coming to the clinic again. The social worker and I tried to explain that no harm would come to Paula from seeing me or the clinic's child therapist and that such meetings could only increase Paula's self-confidence—Mrs P remained firm in her decision, while Paula stayed silent. Finally, and only reluctantly, Mrs P agreed to a follow-up appointment.

The day before the arranged appointment, Mrs P telephoned the clinic and told the social worker that Paula had been very upset ever since our meeting and that she had cried most of the day for several days. Paula had told Mrs P that her tears followed our conversation about her father and his death. Mrs P could see no advantage in this, and, therefore, she did not wish to expose Paula again to such painful experiences. After much discussion, Mrs P did bring Paula the next day. When I saw Paula on her own, she could not speak much, but she made it clear that it was my talking about her father that had so upset her. However much I tried, Paula was no more forthcoming than she had been at our first meeting. I was forced to recognize that we had gone as far as we could. Perhaps Mrs P could not accept further tears and memories about her husband's death, or, perhaps, it was Paula herself that could not cope with the grieving at this point—or, more likely, Paula could never work through her feelings of grief unless she had her mother's understanding and support for this.

When we met Mrs P again, I told her that I would recommend Paula's transfer back to her old school, but I repeated that Paula needed and would benefit from some individual sessions with me or, if she perhaps preferred that Paula should see a woman, with the clinic's child psychotherapist. Mrs P did not see that this would be useful in any way.

Though we had no further contact with Paula or her mother, we learnt from the school that soon after the transfer Paula settled down and became more peaceful and relaxed. For some months, Paula continued to act and dress like a boy, preferring boys' company at playtime, but gradually this subsided, and by the end of two years Paula was behaving like other girls in her class. It was interesting to hear that since returning to her former school, Paula had approached the school nurse and spent considerable time discussing with her the circumstances of her father's death and her feelings about him—something that she had never done before.

Discussion

I would like to think that Paula's interview with me had had a positive therapeutic result. If some might argue that it was the return to her old school that gave Paula the relief from her phobic behaviour, I tend to believe that it was our drawings that enabled her to make such intense and positive use of the school nurse. Mrs P's role is also open to question: are we to think that Paula's delayed grief reaction occurred in spite of and against the opposition of her mother? Or should we assume that, whatever the appearances, Mrs P did allow Paula to cry and, somehow, made it possible for her to find in the school nurse someone who could offer her the support she needed?

It is people like Mrs P who make me think of the biblical Miriam, who ensured that her brother Moses could find someone able to give him the nurturance he needed. Mrs P's refusal to let

Paula attend the child guidance clinic might point to some implied prohibition of Paula's grief, but if this opposition was absolute, then Paula might have remained school-phobic, totally housebound, with no access to any external source of support.

The superimposed drawings and the last squiggles are perhaps the most dramatic examples I have found of such phenomena. Are we to think that these are just interesting coincidences? How can one ever prove that unconscious factors played a definite role in these drawings of Paula's? Having found other examples of similar superimposed images (see, e.g., chapter four, "Georgia", Figure 4.4), I have no doubt that some people can utilize their drawings to convey images that they seem unable to formulate in words or, for that matter, in straightforward single drawings.

CHAPTER SIX

Summing up

Perhaps paradoxically, I want to refer to a child I did not see. Some years ago, a mother telephoned me to ask for help for her daughter, aged 5 years, who presented a severe immune system abnormality. Because this affected not only her skin but also her lungs and other organs, she had required frequent hospitalizations and was under constant medication. The little girl was having individual psychotherapy, and the parents had meetings with a different worker to discuss the child's care. As we discussed the situation and how best to proceed, the mother made a remark that struck me as particularly relevant: "Luckily, my daughter really has no idea of how serious her condition is . . .". After some discussion regarding how the consultation with me would affect the work of the other professionals involved, we made an appointment when I would see the little girl and her parents together, but this was cancelled a few days later.

If the child was under individual therapy and the parents were seeing another worker, what could a joint consultation contribute? I found it remarkable that these parents should believe that their 5-year-old would "have no idea how serious the situation is" after her life-long visits to doctors, intensive and continuous medication, and repeated hospitalizations. Of course, the child might not have a precise notion of the dangers that she was living through, but this presumably would only make matters worse for her, insofar as her fears would have no bounds. If I met this child, I would be able to explore in more detail the nature of her anxieties regarding her illness and treatment, but not having seen the child or the family I was left wondering whether the mother's belief was well founded. On the basis of my experience with other similar cases, I could not dismiss the thought that the mother's words suggested that the child had never found it possible to convey to the parents the nature or the intensity of her fears. I imagine that, probably quite correctly, the child sensed that the parents were already too frightened themselves to cope with further evidence of the suffering she was going through. It is not rare to find this specific brand of "protecting" each other in children with serious physical illnesses. The parents believe they help the child by voicing only words of comfort and encouragement, but the child often interprets this as a sign that the parents cannot cope with hearing of their fears. Indeed, the child might not know how to articulate many of these fears, but what we usually find is a child who (unconsciously) learns to complain only of those symptoms of discomfort and pain that the parents can cope with, and this leads the parents to give further reassurance to the child. I have wondered whether this might set the pattern for some of the cases of psychosomatic illness or hypochondria we find in adults.

Much to parents' surprise, in the protected context of the consultation a child in this situation will gradually find ways of expressing the content of his anxieties (conscious and unconscious). If the parents are also helped to understand their own reasons for not enabling the child to voice his fears and can then address the child differently, a distinct change occurs in the way they interact, and there is no doubt that the parents soon find that their help is more effective.

Children, like all patients (and, in fact, like any person in a position of dependence), have very sensitive antennae to gauge the extent to which they can tax the person on whom they depend. I believe that an extremely subtle exchange of cues occurs between child and parents, exactly as happens between patient and doctor, where each party tries to assess what to say to the other; it can be very difficult for the two parties to ascertain to what extent is their interpretation of the other party's communication correct or, instead, based on their own motives. Seeing the child and the parents together sets up a situation in which they feel protected and manage to tell each other of feelings and thoughts previously kept unspoken; this then helps them to alter a vicious circle in which they had been keeping each other stuck in a web of misconceptions.

Parents, professionals, and all carers do want to believe that their efforts to help are seen as measures stemming exclusively out of concern for the child, patient or whoever needs their ministrations, but how often does this really happen? It is quite puzzling that it should happen so rarely that we professionals should be made to recognize that we are dealing with our own feelings rather than taking into account what the patient is actually concerned with. I learnt this lesson years ago when I was seeing a hospitalized chronic psychotic patient in intensive analytic psychotherapy; as my long-delayed holidays approached, I found myself repeating, in several sessions, the various alternative means through which the patient could obtain help in my absence. After a while my patient smiled and said: "Really, Dr Brafman, you don't have to worry—you can enjoy your holiday, because I know I'll be fine." *Touché*. She was right—I was more worried about the effect of my absence than she was.

More often than we would like to believe, we take a "telling" posture, when in fact the other person would much rather wish we *asked* them for their feelings and views. With children, this happens almost all the time. We tend to know precisely what their problem is, and we are always ready to give them the solution. Some years ago, during a consultation with a family, I was so carried away with my idea that the child's feelings and needs were being ignored by teachers and parents that, when the child mentioned that she sat in the first row of the class, I promptly suggested that here was another example of her having to fight for her needs, that she had found for herself the seat best suited for her eyesight (she wore glasses). She smiled and corrected me: no, she sat in that row because her surname began with the letter "A". I have seen similar assumptions being made in clinical and social settings about a child's behaviour, but it is not often that children manage to feel confident enough to correct the adult's assertions. I can only assume that the child (and the patient) react not only to the words we utter, but that they pick up in our tone of voice whether we expect our words to be taken as gospel or whether we can accept some form of questioning.

Individual therapy is very helpful to the child who has the "average expectable environment" that Winnicott (1971b, p. 5) described as the minimum requirement for normal development. What I have found is that there are many children who have a perfectly "average expectable environment", whose parents would never be considered as, in any way, pathological but who, nevertheless, in some circumstances come to misinterpret the child's words, feelings, or behaviour in such a way that a pathological vicious circle is established, with the child appearing as "the patient".

When there is parental pathology, the gains of individual work with the child become more problematic, though I believe it is still better to offer therapy to the child than leaving child and family without any help. Similarly, if one or both parents need help, it should be offered in some modality that is considered suitable and is acceptable to them. Family therapy is now widely available and offers good results when appropriately indicated. My concern is that because most therapists feel more at home working with adults, the child's personal conflicts tend to be neglected. At best, the child is seen as part of the unit of the family, but not enough attention is given to the child's own perception of the conflicts. The central issue in all these discussions about diagnosis and therapeutic recommendations lies in the decision of what exactly does the child need in order to overcome his difficulties and resume his normal development.

This book aims to illustrate how children can be helped with brief interventions. There is no intention to dismiss or belittle long-term therapy, of whatever kind; the intention, rather, is to argue that intensive and/or extensive therapies should be reserved for those children and adolescents who require them.

Our psychoanalytic upbringing makes no allowances for changes, let alone cures, after brief interventions, but I believe that we still know very little about the pathogenesis of emotional prob-

lems. Some authors point to disturbances in instinctual development, others to pathological object relations, while others point to
neurological or other physical factors, much as behaviourists emphasize learning—no end of theories, but experience with children
can show how frequently a symptom suggesting serious pathology
can disappear after a brief intervention. Resilience? Lifting of defences? Plasticity? My cases point to the depth, intensity, and complexity of the relationship between child and parents—and how,
the younger the child, the easier it seems to be to obtain changes in
the child's feelings and behaviour, as soon as the parents can
modify their perception of the child and, in consequence, treat the
child differently. This is not to say that the parents are the sole
cause of the child's pathological behaviour but, rather, a recognition of the fact that they cannot but treat the child according to how
they came to see themselves as parents and how they perceive the
child himself. The child fits in with this way in which he is treated,
and a vicious circle of interaction is established. If child and parents can understand how they influence each other and manage to
find different ways of living together, these changes can lead them
to a pattern that is more beneficial for the child's development.

There is no doubt that children are resilient. But the word "plasticity" emphasizes their capacity to adapt to the manner in which
they are treated. This is the main challenge for the consultant trying to evaluate a child's behaviour. There is, unfortunately, no
checklist to differentiate a child's reactive behaviour from another
child in whom the same behaviour stems exclusively or predomi-
nantly from factors inherent to the child's psychological make-up.
Assessing parental input and observing the interaction between
child and parents gives us further diagnostic data, as well as allowing us to check how the child responds to any change in the parents' attitudes.

The question remains as to how many interviews are required
for "a proper assessment" of the child's needs. Each worker will
discover his own personal "time requirement", while each institu-
tion tends to decide on a specific length, but the latter, sadly but
predictably, soon turns into a point of dogma. Personally, I approach each case without knowing the length of time I will need
before I feel confident of my opinions. However, time and again I
have found that it is possible to elicit most data I require in one or

two consultations. I have argued that this is because (1) the child, as much as the parents, comes to the interview after a considerable build-up of explicit as well as inarticulated work on the issues that are relevant to "the problem", and (2) I approach the meeting with the goal of discovering the explanation for the presenting problem. If I find that the child is not caught up in, to quote Winnicott (1971b, p. 5), a developmental "knot" but instead requires long-term assistance, this comes to be my recommendation.

Several of the cases described in this book show how the child can benefit from the consultation almost in spite of the parents' contribution, but when the child is very young the long-term prognosis remains doubtful. The younger the child, the more intense is his position of dependence on the parents; if the parents cannot change their approach to the child, I believe that the child has to develop some kind of adaptation that allows them to live together. This may well correspond to Winnicott's description of the "false self" (1960), where the child develops a façade that is acceptable to the parents while learning to repress feelings and behaviours that correspond more closely to his own nature. As mentioned above, I also wonder whether the language of physical and/or specific emotional symptoms can become that person's "language" of expressing distress.

I hope that the work described in this book will inspire others. The number of sessions is not the most important factor, nor is the use of drawings during interviews. These are only examples of a professional attitude of openness, a preparedness to adapt to the real capacities and needs of the child who comes to us seeking help. Like all professionals, I do have preconceptions (see chapter one) regarding the mechanisms that lead a normally developing child to present behaviour we call "pathological", but these theoretical assumptions still allow me the latitude to explore the specific characteristics of each individual child; then, taking into account each parent's ability to adapt to the child's needs, I gradually come to decide how best to help the child. If one or a few meetings helps them to build on any initial gains and then to carry on without my participation, I count this as a success—for all of us.

REFERENCES

Accioly Lins, M. I. (1990). The squiggle game. *Rev. Bras. Psicanálise, 24* (2).

Brafman, A. H. (1997). Winnicott's *Therapeutic Consultations* revisited. *International Journal of Psycho-Analysis, 78*: 773–787.

Brafman, A. H. (1999). Taking advantage of the mutual influences between parents and children. *Rev. Bras. Psicanálise, 33* (2): 339–361.

Farhi, N. (1996). "Psychotherapy and the Squiggle Game: 'A Sophisticated Game of Hide and Seek'." Unpublished paper read at a meeting of the Squiggle Foundation, 26 June.

Fraiberg, S. (1980). *Clinical Studies in Infant Mental Health*. London: Tavistock Publications.

Freud, S. (1910). "Wild" psycho-analysis. *S.E., 11*, pp. 219–227.

Gampel, Y. (1995). The second *Bedeutung* of the *Deutung*. *Psychoanalysis in Europe, 45*: 42–67.

Phillips, A. (1988). *Winnicott*. London: Fontana.

Winnicott, D. W. (1956). The antisocial tendency. In: *Through Paediatrics to Psycho-Analysis* (pp. 306–315). London: Tavistock, 1958. [Reprinted London: Hogarth Press, 1975; reprinted London: Karnac Books, 1992.]

Winnicott, D. W. (1960). Ego distortion in terms of true self and false self. In: *The Maturational Processes and the Facilitating Environment* (pp. 140–152). London: Hogarth Press, 1965. [Reprinted London: Karnac Books, 1990.]

Winnicott, D. W. (1971a). *Playing and Reality*. London: Tavistock, 1971.

Winnicott, D. W. (1971b). *Therapeutic Consultations in Child Psychiatry*. London: Hogarth Press.

INDEX

Acciolly Lins, M. I., 39
aggressive behaviour, 71–75
"Angela", 48, 50–57
anorexia nervosa, 28
"antisocial tendency" (Winnicott), 3,
    12
anxieties:
    of child, sexual content to, 99
    and confusion, over bodily
        functions, 117–120
    parental, 55–57
    of seriously ill child, 155–156
    in young child, 62–71
assessment, length of, 159–160
attitude of parents, and behaviour of
    child, 73–74
aural hallucinations, 28, 34–35
"average expectable environment"
    (Winnicott), 3, 9, 158

bedwetting/enuresis, 33, 34, 48–49,
    58–62, 79, 82–86, 88–91, 112,
    143. See also bladder control
behaviour:
    aggressive, 71–75
    pathological, 160
    unconscious motivation for, 49
bereavement, 113, 120
bladder control, 49, 57–61, 62–71, 79.
    See also bedwetting
"Bob", 48–49, 57–62

body image and body functions of
    child, linked to mother's
    pathology, 110
bowel dysfunction, 75–80. See also
    sphincter dysfunction
Brafman, A. H., 26, 28, 34, 121

Caldwell, P., 40
case studies:
    "Angela", 48, 50–57
    "Bob", 48–49, 57–62
    "Claude", 49, 62–71
    "Daniel", 49, 71–75
    "David" , 26, 34
    "Edward", 49–50, 75–80
    "Gamal", 28, 34
    "Georgia", 20, 38, 95–104, 154
    "Harriet", 96, 104–110
    "Jane", 34, 50, 80–92
    "Leon", 96, 110–121, 123
    "Mary", 123, 124–136
    "Paula" , 26, 38, 124, 141–153
    "Penny", 121
    "Trevor", 124, 136–141
castration anxiety, 70
child:
    ability of to express fears during
        consultation, 156
    and achieving independence, 57
    assessment of development of, 16
    awareness of need for help, 13

body image and body functions of,
    and pathology of mother, 110
and childbirth, understanding of,
    117–118
and conflicting injunctions from
    parents, 73–74
and conversations between
    therapist and parents, 20–21,
    53, 56, 68, 71, 76–77
developing relationship with, 15–
    16
distress of, communicated through
    physical complaints, 80
effect of attitude towards, 29
emotional dependence on mother,
    93
engaging with, 14–15
expecting help from consultant,
    135–136
feedback from, on interpretations,
    18–19
hostility towards mother, revealed
    through drawings, 133, 135
mute, 44
parental perception of, 159
parents' attitude towards, 36
physical symptomatology of, as
    language learnt from parents,
    80
preconceived notion of consultant,
    8, 12, 121
reaction of to advice from parents,
    24
relationship of to father, 136–141
resentment of towards mother, 38
"rights of", 29
sensitivity of, to limits of
    dependency for support, 156–
    157
symptoms of, originating from
    treatment by parents, 22–23
unspoken communications of,
    verbalizing, 5
childbirth, child's understanding of,
    117–118
"Claude", 49, 62–71
communication, through play, 78–80
consultant:
    ability of to draw, 41
    child's formation of relationship
        with before therapy, 8, 12, 121

developing relationship with child,
    15–16
influence of on patients, 43
personal attributes of, 17
principles guiding work, 31–32
psychopathology of, 42
seen by child as potential helper, 79
consultation, 30–33, 39–45
    diagnostic, 3
    engaging the child, 25
    initial, 13–14
    joint, 155–156
    as opportunity for child to "open
        up", 24
    therapeutic, 2, 5–9, 12, 16, 19, 33–
        37, 39
countertransference, 41–42

"Daniel", 49, 71–75
"David" , 26, 34
development, emotional and
    physical, and diagnostic
    evaluation, 4–5
developmental milestones/stages, 16,
    26, 29, 33, 34, 37, 75
diagnostic assessment, 31, 33
    and emotional and physical
        development, 4–5
    length of, 159–160
discipline:
    conflict between parents
        regarding, 125, 133, 135
    lack of, 59, 112
doctors, over-attachment to, 107
drawings, 19–20, 44–45, 84–86, 90,
    108, 113–119, 127–132, 139–
    141, 144–147
    by child, hostility towards mother,
        revealed through, 133
    communication through, 132, 134–
        135
    as expression of feelings, 87, 88–89,
        108, 110
    as language to convey thoughts
        and feelings, 37–38
    as means of conveying
        experiences, 54–55
    by mother, to child's instructions,
        67–68
    related to real-life events, 121, 140–
        141

drawings (*continued*):
　　and retrieval of lost memories, 99
　　by therapist, 41:
　　　　influence of interpretations on,
　　　　　　42
　　　　influence of on child, 42
　　　　of traumatic event, 99–104
　　　　verbalization through, 140, 154
dream(s), 8, 56, 123, 133
　　articulated through play, 52–53
　　as clue to unconscious fantasy, 8
　　see also nightmares, sleep
　　　　disturbance

eating problems, 50
educational difficulties, 142–143, 152–
　　153
"Edward", 49–50, 75–80
emotion, suppressed, 144–147, 152
emotional contact, importance of
　　establishing with child, 44
emotional dependence of child on
　　mother, 93
emotional development, of child, 18
emotional disturbance, pathogenesis
　　of, 158–159
enuresis, 33, 49, 70, 79, 112, 143. *See
　　also* bedwetting

"false self" (Winnicott), 79, 160
family:
　　background of, 25–26, 29–30
　　lack of discipline, 112
　　pathology of, 26
fantasy, sexual, 101
Farhi, N., 40
father:
　　death of, 142, 143, 144, 152–153
　　involvement of in consultation,
　　　　136–141
follow-up meeting, 36–37, 53, 57, 92,
　　104, 134, 136
Fraiberg, S., 22
Freud, S., 1, 3

"Gamal", 28, 34
Gampel, Y., 39
gender identity, 143, 144, 145, 153
"Georgia", 20, 38, 95–104, 154
"ghosts in the nursery" (Fraiberg), 22
guilt, of parents, 26

hallucinations, aural, 28, 34–35
"Harriet", 96, 104–110
Hood, J., 40

"illness", model of, avoiding, 61
images, superimposed, 38–39. *See also*
　　superimposed pictures
independence, from parents, 57
initial consultation:
　　participation of parents in, 27–28
　　presence of parents at, 23–24
interpretations:
　　disputed, 83–84, 91
　　negative response of mother to,
　　　　126, 132–136
　　reaction of parents to, 35

"Jane", 34, 50, 80–92

"knot", developmental (Winnicott),
　　27, 35, 160

"Leon", 96, 110–121, 123
listening, 18

"Mary", 123, 124–136
memories, lost, retrieved through
　　drawings, 99
"Miriam's syndrome", 30
"mixed messages", 49
mother:
　　–daughter relationship, 50
　　emotional dependence of child on,
　　　　93
　　negative response of to
　　　　interpretations, 126, 132–136
　　resentment of child towards, 38
Munchausen-by-proxy syndrome, 12

nightmares, 34, 52, 55, 97–98, 103,
　　123, 124, 126, 133, 134, 136

object relations, 3, 19, 26–27, 30, 159

parent(s):
　　absence of, and crisis in child, 69
　　active involvement of in
　　　　consultation, 47–93
　　as agent for improvement of
　　　　child's problems, 23
　　attitude of towards child, 36

background of, 111–112
    and problems of child, 72
capacity of to offer environmental
    provisions, 5, 9
and child, mutual influence of, 2
childhood experiences of, 120
–child interaction, assessing, 160
–child relationship, pathological,
    158, 159, 160
conflicting signals from, to child,
    73
as effective helpers of child, 28–29
engaging with, 14–15
guilt, 26
inability of to help child overcome
    problem, 27, 156
influence of, on child's problems,
    10, 12–13
influence of child's therapy on, 49
involvement in therapeutic
    intervention, 2
lack of support for child 92–93
pathological behaviour of, 23, 158
perception of child's problems, 35,
    159
problems of, affecting child, 27, 28
prominent role of, in therapy of
    child, 9–10
psychopathology of, 21–22
reactions of:
    to child's drawings, 20–21
    to child's problems, 24
    to child's statements during
        consultation, 24–25
    to consultant's interpretations,
        35, 126, 132–136
role of in joint interview, 95–121
seeking background accounts
    from, 25–26
self-centred, 15
"Paula" , 26, 38, 124, 141–153
"Penny", 121
phallic rivalry, 38
Phillips, A., 6
phobias, 50–55
physical complaints, as
    communication of distress, 80
physical symptomatology, of child, as
    language learnt from parents,
    80
play, during consultation, 126–127

materials, 19–20
    choice of, 45
presenting problem, 27, 28, 33–34, 35,
    36, 160
problems, transgenerational, 34
psyche:
    of child, 22
    of the individual, 1–2
    of therapist, and drawings, 41–42
psychotherapy:
    length of, 3–4
    vs. psychoanalysis, decision
        concerning, 3–4, 7

referral, 30–31, 34, 50–51, 62–63, 75–
    76, 80–81, 97, 105, 110–111,
    124–125, 136, 137
repetitive behaviours, 49

school:
    attendance problems, 142
    difficulties at, 55, 57, 141, 153
self-confidence, building, 61
self-control, lack of, 48–49, 60, 62
self-esteem, 34
siblings, 15, 59, 112, 136–137
    birth of, 126, 135
    threat from, 92
sleep:
    disturbance, 53, 88, 97, 124–126,
        136–141
    -walking, 97
speech difficulties, 34
sphincter dysfunction, 77, 89, 96, 105–
    121:
    and bowel habits of parents, 106–
        107
    parental reaction to, 113
squiggle game, 32, 37–38, 39–45, 147–
    152
    description of, 7–8
    as means of communicating with
        children, 6
    objections to, 40–41
    as part of diagnostic assessment,
        40
superimposed pictures, 38–39, 95–96,
    102–103, 124, 147, 154
symptom, 24, 26, 36, 79
    of child, originating in parents'
        treatment of, 22–23

symptom (*continued*):
    different reactions of professionals
        to, 134
    and family dynamics, 62
    as means of conveying feelings, 86,
        89
    perpetuation of, 36
    as plea for help, 11–12
    presenting, 27, 28
    as response to parent's needs, 12
    transgenerational, 112, 113, 120

therapeutic consultation (Winnicott),
        2, 59, 12, 16, 19, 32, 33–37, 39
therapy:
    long-term, 36–37
    parental influence on, 49–50
toilet training, 62–71
transgenerational problems, 83–84,
        89, 112, 113, 120
"Trevor", 124, 136–141
trust, 17

unconscious anxieties:
    expressed through play, 79
    verbalized, 135
unconscious fantasies, 7, 8, 9, 18, 19,
        24, 35, 36, 42, 62, 121
    elucidation of through drawings,
        37–39

verbalization, of child's unspoken
    communications, 5

Winnicott, 2–10, 16, 121
    antisocial tendency, 3, 12
    approach of, 31–32
    attitude towards parents, 9
    average expectable environment,
        3, 158
    facilitating environment, 19
    false self, 79, 160
    holding environment, 3
    knot, developmental, 27, 160
    mothers:
        good-enough, 3, 19
        importance of , 21–22
    object-relations theory, 3
    Playing and Reality, 21
    sacred moment, 16–17, 19
    seen in child's dreams, 8, 12
    squiggle game, 39–45
        description of, 7–8
        as means of communicating
            with children, 6
        objections to, 40–41
        as part of diagnostic
            assessment, 40
    therapeutic consultation, 2, 59, 12,
        16, 19, 32, 33–37, 39
        length of, 3–4, 5
    *Therapeutic Consultations in Child
        Psychiatry*, 5–7
    and unconscious conflicts, 6
    use of an object, 19

words, limitations of, 19–20